EMPOWER YOUR

WEALTH.

Empower Your Wealth

TAKE CHARGE OF YOUR FINANCIAL FUTURE BY
BUILDING THE MILLIONAIRE MINDSET AND
ADOPTING WEALTH HABITS FOR LIVING A RICH LIFE

Scott Allan

Scott Allan S A
PUBLISHING
ONE BOOK AT A TIME

Copyright page

Table of Contents

"You either master money, or, on some level, money masters you."

– **Tony Robbins,** bestselling author of Money: Master the Game

Empower Your Wealth: The Introduction

If you often struggle to attract wealth and abundance, please read this book because what you learn here could change your life in unimaginable ways.

We all want to live happy, balanced, successful lives full of wealth and abundance. We want to be rich. We want to prosper in life. And we want to live life on our terms.

Many of us fall short of achieving what we want, only to complain about the struggle while rarely reflecting on the root cause of the problem. The inability to attract abundance and wealth boils down to not having the right beliefs. That's why true abundance and wealth always begins with self-empowerment.

Empower Your Wealth is no ordinary book. This guide will redefine your concept, perception and understanding of wealth and abundance.

Unlike conventional financial and money management guides, this book focuses on reshaping your beliefs, thoughts, attitudes and actions to foster a mindset of abundance and wealth attraction.

This is important because the results we get in life, whether it is achieving our financial goals, building healthy relationships, improving a particular behavior, becoming healthy, or anything else, are directly related to our beliefs in that area.

For example, if you want to become healthier and lose weight, your beliefs about health and fitness must be positive, healthy, and productivity-oriented. Similarly, if you want to live a happy, passionate life with your spouse, your beliefs need to be relationship-centered.

The same is true for wealth and abundance. To be wealthy in the most authentic sense, you must cultivate a mindset that attracts wealth and abundance.

Empower Your Wealth takes you on a journey of exploring and discovering your beliefs about wealth and abundance. It encourages you to perceive wealth in terms of financial abundance and as a unique blend of spiritual, emotional, and intellectual prosperity.

As you progress through the guide, you will begin to break the shackles of the limiting beliefs and scarcity mindset that keep you from becoming wealthy and prosperous. You will also successfully replace them with an abundance mindset that is a magnet for wealth in all its forms.

Empower Your Wealth is like a compass that points you to the right beliefs that will help you attract exactly the kind of wealth you want and the abundance the universe is eager to give you. The book is full of actionable exercises, tactics, and strategies designed to help you do what you need to do to fix your wealth and abundance mindset. We will also use real-life examples to help you identify and effectively use your strengths and passions.

In addition, this book will provide you with strategies for building and growing relationships that foster wealth. By the time you turn the final page of this wealth blueprint, you will have a clear vision and action plan for cultivating and maintaining a healthy life while accumulating abundance and wealth. You'll learn to cultivate an attitude of gratitude, harness the power of visualization, use affirmations, and adopt the habits of the wealthy to attract wealth to you.

A unique feature of the book is its comprehensive concept and approach to strengthening your wealth while giving you nuggets of information and strategies.

If you want to start manifesting wealth and abundance from the ground up, this book is for you. And if you want to improve a particular aspect of wealth, this book is for you too. You can read it from start to finish, or you can skip certain chapters and go to the parts that focus on the area you want to improve.

What This Book Will Teach You:

Empower Your Wealth is a comprehensive guide designed to help you unlock your true potential and truly empower your wealth and abundance. It aims to achieve this goal by providing accurate guidance and actionable strategies on various aspects of wealth.

After reading this book, you'll emerge as a more focused, grateful, and powerful individual who knows exactly what kind of wealth he/she wants.

In this book, you'll discover:

✓ 11 comprehensive chapters on wealth and abundance to transform your understanding of wealth.

- ✓ Guidelines for overcoming the scarcity mindset and limiting beliefs that hinder your potential for wealth creation and accumulation.
- ✓ Actionable techniques to help you leverage your unique strengths and passions to unlock your wealth potential.
- ✓ Practical exercises for cultivating gratitude, harnessing the power of visualization, and creating personal wealth affirmations.
- ✓ Secrets for adopting the habits of the wealthy and creating value to accumulate wealth.
- ✓ Tactics for building and maintaining meaningful and profitable relationships that promote wealth creation.
- ✓ Steps and exercises for creating your personal wealth vision and strategy while maintaining a balanced and fulfilling life.
- ✓ A deeper understanding for the importance of resilience and continuous learning in your journey to wealth.

Take it one page and one chapter at a time and you will complete the entire book. Believe me, it is very easy.

Even if you think reading is easy and implementing what you read into your life is difficult, it is not.

Empower Your Wealth is your roadmap to creating abundance and wealth in the most authentic sense and way possible so that you can live a rich, meaningful and balanced life in every way possible.

Let's begin this journey towards transformational wealth and abundance.

Scott Allan **S** **A**
B O O K S

MASTER YOUR LIFE
ONE BOOK AT A TIME

"Formal education will make you a living; self-education will make you a fortune."

— **Jim Rohn,** entrepreneur and motivational speaker

Chapter 1:
Rethinking Wealth

'The real measure of our wealth is how much we'd be worth if we lost all our money.'
—John Henry Jowett

I want you to read that quote twice and think about what you would be worth if you didn't have a single penny in your name or on your person. That sounds strange to even imagine, right?

Well, it clearly shows that the beliefs we have held about wealth are inaccurate. Many of us perceive wealth and abundance in terms of money. Yes, wealth includes financial gain, but it's not all about that.

A major reason many of us consistently fail to become as wealthy as we want to be is that we hold unhealthy and limiting beliefs about wealth and abundance.

Since the solution to any problem begins with the correct diagnosis of the problem, you must begin to rethink what you think and believe about wealth if you truly want to become wealthy.

Traditional Perceptions and Beliefs About Wealth

Traditionally, when we talk about wealth and abundance, we think primarily in terms of money and material possessions. We consider someone with more money to be wealthier than someone with less money. We usually perceive wealth in terms of having more of everything: bigger houses, more cars, more possessions, more real estate, bigger bank accounts, and more luxurious vacations.

We also seem to believe that those who want more money are selfish. There is a lot of stigma attached to the desire to get rich, and we often label people who want to get rich as materialistic.

Many of us use money as a critical factor in determining our success or failure. If you make more money, you are successful. Unfortunately, if you don't make enough money to be considered successful by society, you get the badge of failure.

We also seem to believe that getting rich isn't easy. We often throw around the old adage, "money doesn't grow on trees" in discussions about wealth and money. People think that you have to work extraordinarily hard to become wealthy.

We also seem to believe that to be wealthy you have to be frugal. If you keep spending, you will never get rich, because "saving" is the common mantra for making more money.

Another traditional view of wealth is that it is the root of all evil. Having more money is often associated with a tendency to be materialistic. And, those who struggle to be wealthy often complain that since their ancestors were poor, they are likely to be poor as well.

Unfortunately, all of these perceptions are usually just that: perceptions that do not represent reality. These perceptions can keep you from becoming wealthy and attracting abundance. But don't worry, we're going to challenge and reframe them in this book, so keep reading.

The Right Concept of Wealth

Like success and happiness, wealth is a very relative term. Its definition and meaning vary from person to person.

For some people, wealth is entirely monetary. It refers to what you can buy with your money. For others, however, wealth goes beyond the money in their bank account. For them, wealth is mainly about having flexibility and freedom in life.

Yes, monetary wealth measures the value of everything you own. So all of your assets play a role in determining your wealth. But in reality, wealth goes much further than that.

Wealth is determined by how rich and generous you are in your mind and heart. True wealth goes beyond what is in your pocket and bank account. It is about knowing that you can attract whatever you want.

In essence, true wealth is about achieving freedom.

According to Michael Berkhahn, a renowned financial planner, "Wealth is when someone has financial freedom through all economic cycles."

If we focus on Berkhahn's definition, we will realize that wealth is more about not feeling stressed. Wealth and abundance aren't necessarily about owning and having more. It is about feeling free and having the independence and flexibility to live the way you want. It also refers to not feeling paralyzed when the economy goes through a downturn.

If you focus more on having lots of luxurious and expensive things, you are trying to become financially wealthy.

However, it's important that you also focus on the intangibles associated with true wealth. These include freedom, flexibility, serenity, gratitude, and cultivating a growth mindset. When you know you have a rich heart and are grateful for your wealth, you automatically begin to feel wealthy.

In reality, wealth in its truest sense refers to wealth emotionally, spiritually, and intellectually. It goes beyond having more stuff and being financially rich.

Having a Rich Heart and Gratitude to Attain Wealth

When we cultivate or focus on having a rich heart, we experience the profound effect of gratitude on our perception of wealth.

A rich heart is not about material possessions, but about the abundance of love, kindness, and generosity we hold within. It's about enriching our lives with meaningful relationships, experiences, and a sense of purpose that can transcend the superficial appeal of material wealth. This in turn attracts abundance into our reality in a holistic sense.

Gratitude plays a central role in this journey. When we truly appreciate what we have, regardless of its size or value, we shift our focus from scarcity to abundance.

This shift in perspective is powerful; it fosters contentment and joy, which I believe are the true hallmarks of an abundant life. By being grateful for our current abundance—whether it is our health, family, friends, or even small daily comforts—we begin to attract more positivity into our lives.

In the chapters that follow, we explore in depth the profound effect that shifting our focus from scarcity to abundance has on attracting abundance into our human experience.

The attitude of gratitude and the abundance of the heart create a virtuous cycle. It drives us to share our wealth with others, not only in monetary terms, but also through acts of kindness and support.

As we give, we receive; not only do we enrich the lives of others, but we also increase our own sense of abundance and fulfillment. The act of giving is so important in wealth empowerment—not only because we touch the lives of those around us—but also because it reaffirms to us that we have enough wealth for ourselves and others.

Moreover, as you will learn more about in this book, feeling wealthy is not only a state of mind, but also a catalyst for actual wealth creation. When we shift our mindset from one of scarcity to one of gratitude and abundance, we are more likely to take calculated risks, seize opportunities, and work toward our goals with optimism and resilience. This proactive approach can ultimately lead to financial abundance.

In essence, having a rich heart and feeling grateful are not just moral virtues, but practical strategies for living a fulfilled life and achieving true wealth. This book will provide you with the actionable steps and practices to elevate your thinking and your wealth.

Being wealthy and abundant means knowing the kind of life you want to live, and being grateful for what you have. Many of us continue to live meaningless lives and complain about it. We want more money, but we fail to attract it. This happens because we are unclear about the kind of money and life we want.

Perhaps wealth is pouring into your life in the form of gifts from others, but you want your bank account to get fatter. Maybe you are getting great opportunities to attract abundance, but you keep turning them down because you are doing things that you like.

Abundance is about being free and independent to do what you want and be who you want. It comes from building a strong, positive mindset based on attracting wealth and abundance into your life.

When I call this book your wealth creation compass, I really mean it. This book will educate you about wealth creation and give you practical ways to materialize it.

When you start implementing the small tactics discussed in this book, you will be amazed at how easily you can manifest the wealth and abundance you have always wanted.

"When you understand that your self-worth is not determined by your net-worth, then you'll have financial freedom."

— **Suze Orman**

Chapter 2:
Wealth—More Than Just Money

'It is the heart that makes a man rich. He is rich according to what he is, not according to what he has.'
— *Henry Ward Beecher*

For many of us, wealth is just about money. In reality, wealth is an all-encompassing phenomenon. And it is more than a concept. It has different dimensions, and only by understanding the different dimensions can you fully grasp the true concept of wealth.

If creating wealth is a big struggle for you, it is probably because you have not yet understood wealth. So, why don't we clarify what it truly means right here and right now.

The Different Dimensions of Wealth
Wealth goes beyond the material realm. You may find this surprising, but wealth has various physical, mental, emotional, intellectual, psychological, and spiritual dimensions.

Physical Wealth
Physical wealth is what many people call the "material" aspect of wealth. It includes your physical health and financial wealth.

You are probably already familiar with financial wealth, including your money, financial resources, buildings, cars, houses, furniture, devices, and other material assets. But that is just the tip of the wealth iceberg.

Physical wealth is your physical health. If you are physically fit and healthy, you have physical wealth. Physical health is critical to creating and accumulating wealth because you cannot work to earn money and build your wealth without a healthy and functioning body and mind.

Think of it this way—you may want to become a millionaire and own a digital marketing company, but if you keep getting sick, you will not be able to achieve your goal, right? So, your physical well-being is crucial to creating the material wealth you want.

Moreover, physical wealth is important not only to create wealth, but also to enjoy it. What good is your success if you are lying in bed and cannot celebrate it? A healthy and active body is essential for creating and celebrating wealth.

Spiritual Wealth

Spiritual wealth is related to your spirituality. Spirituality is a very relative term, meaning it can mean different things to different people.

But if you dig deep into its various interpretations, they boil down to one thing: **having a sense of purpose and direction in life.**

So, your spirituality is having a clear sense of purpose in life. To be spiritual, you must focus on discovering what you are meant to do. When you explore your spirituality, you get a sense of purpose in life.

Your life becomes meaningful, and instead of spending your time doing meaningless things that appeal to you, you focus primarily on what drives you to create a healthy life.

Spiritual wealth is about finding your spirituality and infusing it with a sense of passion, purpose and motivation. When you are spiritually wealthy, you have clarity about your vision and mission in life. You know exactly what you need to do to live a fulfilling and thriving life that makes you happy and creates value for others.

Let me share a story with you. President John F. Kennedy was touring NASA headquarters in 1961. During his tour, he came across a janitor who was busily cleaning the floor. Since it was late, the president asked the janitor why he was working so late.

The janitor could have responded as most people would in this situation: "I'm cleaning the floor because that's my job," or "My supervisor asked me to work late today," "Because that's my job," or something along those lines.

Instead, he calmly replied, "I'm helping to put a man on the moon." His answer came as quite a surprise to President Kennedy. At the same time, it conveyed to him the janitor's dedication to his work and his clarity about his life's purpose.

For this janitor, mopping floors was not a menial task. To him, it was doing his part to make it easier for the scientists, researchers, and astronauts to achieve their goals and improve the nation's economy.

Every time I write about or read this story, It is a wake up call. It is a perfect example of the magic of spiritual wealth. This janitor was not rich in money. But he was rich in spiritual wealth, which gave him the greatest satisfaction and fulfillment.

Emotional Wealth

When we talk about wealth, we tend to overlook its emotional aspect.

Emotional wealth refers to being emotionally wealthy. It is about your ability to feel and experience your emotions and to regulate them effectively.

When you are emotionally wealthy, you can distinguish between healthy and unhealthy emotions. You also know how to deal with intense emotions that can become overwhelming and disturb your mental peace. Emotional wealth also equips you with the ability to cultivate healthy emotions that you can use to your advantage.

Having emotional wealth allows you to connect with and understand your emotions. There are many ups and downs in life. Each time adversity hits you, you are likely to be off balance for some time. If you don't have emotional wealth, chances are you will allow strong, negative emotions such as sadness, grief, frustration and disappointment to take over. When this happens, you may find it difficult to get back on track.

On the other hand, being emotionally wealthy allows you to keep your emotions in check and manage them successfully. It is not that you do not experience such emotions. Of course you do, but you know how to control them instead of letting them get the best of you.

In addition to helping you bounce back from problems, emotional wealth enables you to use positive emotions to your advantage. Sometimes, when we experience a strong positive emotion, it causes us to make impulsive decisions. For example, you may agree to a job opportunity because you got it and it pays well. However, when you think about it later, you realize that it does not align with your purpose in life.

Adopting a mindset of emotional wealth makes it easy to regulate such positive emotions, which helps you make more informed and fruitful decisions in life, including those about financial wealth.

Emotional wealth also helps you connect with people more easily and on a deeper level. You find it easy to connect with others, to understand them, and to build meaningful, happy relationships.

Someone who is emotionally wealthy finds it easy to stay positive, fight life's obstacles, find happiness on their own, be happy for others, and emotionally support others in difficult times.

Intellectual Wealth

Intellectual wealth refers to the skills, expertise and knowledge you possess. It is what you have gained from all the education you have acquired in your life, the experience you have had while doing any professional work, and any training you have gone through.

Simply put, all of your knowledge and expertise helps you create and acquire material assets, also known as material wealth.

It covers many areas of knowledge, including creativity, business acumen, analytical and critical thinking, technical expertise, and problem-solving skills. Organizations and individuals need intellectual capital to improve productivity, advance careers, grow businesses, drive innovation, and gain a competitive advantage.

If you are knowledgeable about marketing and business, work for a marketing firm, or run your own marketing business, your knowledge, skills, and expertise constitute your intellectual capital. Similarly, an athlete who runs marathons has intellectual wealth related to his or her field.

Intellectual wealth also extends beyond your professional and career-based knowledge and expertise. Throughout your life, from the time you opened your eyes to the world until now, you have learned a thing or two about the world, right? You have to understand how to interact with people, build relationships, take care of your health, build a career, and so on. All this also forms your intellectual wealth.

We need intellectual wealth to keep learning, growing, and adapting to our challenges and experiences. It allows us to move forward, build and excel in our careers, and create the life we want.

Psychological Wealth

Happiness: "Unlocking the Mysteries of Psychological Wealth" is a popular research paper by researchers Robert-Biswas-Diener and Ed Diener. It explores the concept of psychological wealth.

According to the researchers, psychological wealth refers to your overall well-being and the richness of your emotional and spiritual life. It consists of your emotional well-being, your sense of resilience, your ability to form and maintain relationships, and your ability to be mindful and aware. Psychological wealth also includes your level of satisfaction and fulfillment in life.

You find it easy to stay calm and composed when you have psychological wealth. You also remain steadfast when problems come your way and know how to deal with them.

You also understand that happiness is a choice, and you know how to make that choice. You are also able to create healthy and thriving relationships. In addition, you feel at peace with where you are in life and have a high sense of fulfillment as a result.

You have control and autonomy over your life, allowing you to live on your own terms.

Social Wealth

Your social wealth is about the relationships and social contacts you have in your life.

The relationships in your life play a monumental role in determining the quality of your life. You will automatically feel peaceful if you are surrounded by healthy, happy, balanced relationships.

Knowing that you have a loving partner, children who respect and love you, and a family that always supports you is a wonderful blessing. That is certainly wealth in itself.

Social wealth also extends beyond personal relationships and includes social acquaintances, networks, and contacts that add value to your life. Having a healthy relationship with your boss and colleagues, and being connected to influential people with autonomy and influence, brings authority and power into your life.

They also help you identify, and take advantage of, various profitable opportunities. A friend of mine had a very large social circle. He knew a lot of people, which often helped him find many profitable opportunities. Once, he wanted to open a branch of his shoe store in Malaysia, but he could not move forward with this plan. After working on the idea for about a month, he met a businessman from Malaysia at another friend's social gathering. One thing led to another, and the two worked together to open a shoe store in Malaysia.

In addition, influential people can often help with difficult tasks without much effort. For example, you may need information from the Food and Drug Administration for your thesis research. You keep calling and visiting the department, but you cannot find anyone to help you.

In this scenario, if you have a friend who works there or knows someone who does, you can use their influence to get the information you need quickly and conveniently.

Social wealth is often a much more valuable and meaningful component of wealth than financial resources.

The interconnectedness of different forms of wealth

All types of wealth are interconnected. To be truly wealthy, you must have all of these dimensions of wealth in your life.

Let's explore their interconnectedness in this part of the book.

Physical wealth, both your physical health and your financial resources, is critical to your survival. As you know, you need money and a healthy body and mind to meet your needs in life.

Without money, you cannot have a roof over your head, food on the table, and clothes to wear. So, a certain amount of money is important and necessary to meet your basic physiological needs.

Your physical health is also essential to thrive in life. You cannot enjoy life if you are sick most of the time. Just as you need physical health and money to meet your basic needs, you need love and relationships to meet your emotional needs.

Human beings are social creatures. We have an innate need to love and be loved. We also need support, comfort, admiration, and care to feel good about ourselves and be happy from within. This is where your relational/social wealth comes in. You feel emotionally stable and secure when family and friends show you affection and care.

Then, you have people to share your joys with and to lean on when sorrows hit hard. A support system helps you get through difficult times, encourages you to pursue and achieve your goals, and provides a great deal of health. As a result, you will find it easier to focus on your plans and activities to create financial wealth.

In addition, when you are surrounded by love and joy, your emotional and mental health improves, which automatically improves your physical well-being. You function optimally and easily pursue your wealth creation goals when you feel mentally and physically fit.

The other aspect of social wealth is equally important in helping you create and accumulate wealth. Motivational speakers and business gurus often say, "Your network is your net worth."

Having good, powerful, knowledgeable and influential people in your social circle helps you leverage their skills, abilities, intellect, power and money. This opens doors of opportunity that can often make it much easier for you to get closer to your goals.

For example, consider this scenario to help you understand the importance of social wealth in your life and how it relates to financial wealth.

Suppose you want to start a drop-shipping business, but you need guidance and good vendors. If you have people in your social circle—and even family who run a drop-shipping business, or know people in that business—they can help you. Your role in this equation is that you have made some good connections and now, their expertise is helping you get closer to your goal.

The Power of Social Wealth

Your social wealth helps you create and accumulate more financial wealth. Your emotional wealth is very close and important to your financial and physical wealth.

First, when you are in touch with your emotions, you understand yourself better and how different things affect you. With this knowledge, you can make various positive improvements to yourself. For example, if you notice that you often lose your temper, you can dig deeper and realize that you have an anger management problem. This could also be affecting your professional relationships at work and your interpersonal relationships.

So, you start working on the problem to improve it. As your anger issues improve, so does your ability to work with others in your workplace. You begin to build warm and comfortable relationships with your co-workers and supervisors, which also helps you perform better at work. This helps you to do better financially over time.

In addition, as your emotional wealth improves, your relationships become stronger and healthier. Your loved ones like you better than before, and your life becomes happier. And with a more stable and peaceful mind comes the ability to effectively work on and achieve your goals.

Emotional wealth is also strongly related to your spiritual, intellectual and psychological wealth. The four are very closely related.

Spirituality comes from thinking about yourself and what you want. If your emotions are all over the place and you have trouble understanding them, you will find it difficult to focus on your spirituality.

As you gain more emotional wealth, it becomes easier to understand and manage your emotions. You also begin to spend more time reflecting on yourself. Introspection leads to self-discovery, which helps you gradually find your purpose in life and gain spiritual wealth.

Finding your purpose in life helps you to align your attitudes, behaviors, actions, and activities with it. Thus, you begin to work on acquiring the skills and expertise necessary to approach and fulfill your purpose, so that my friend can help you build spiritual wealth.

As your intellectual, emotional, spiritual, and other aspects of wealth improve, your psychological wealth improves. You build the grit and perseverance necessary to face life's challenges and still move toward your purpose.

That's basically how all the different types of wealth are related. To be truly wealthy, you need to work on cultivating these different types of wealth. Let's talk more about that in the next chapter.

Chapter 3:
How to Cultivate the Different Forms of Wealth

"We make a living by what we get,
but we make a life by what we give."
– Winston Churchill

Good health is a blessing. Remember the old saying, "Health is wealth"? The good news is that you can create this blessing for yourself. Yes, some people are born with congenital disorders (some of them even life-threatening) that they cannot do anything about. But you can create physical wealth.

Here's how to do it: Start by establishing your sleep routine. A good night's sleep does wonders for your body and mind. It improves your memory and cognition, boosts your creativity, strengthens your immune system, and regulates your emotions. It also helps you manage your weight, lowers your risk of heart disease and diabetes, and reduces stress.

So yes, you do need a good night's sleep. According to the American Sleep Association, adults need an average of 7 to 9 hours of sleep a night to function optimally. If you are sleeping fewer hours, improve your sleep routine to establish your sleep cycle.

A golden rule is to set a consistent bedtime and wake-up time. The two times should be such that you get at least 7 to 9 hours of sleep. Make sure you go to bed without your phone at least 20 minutes before your bedtime so you can relax and begin to fall asleep.

At first, you may not fall asleep easily and may toss and turn a lot. But soon your circadian rhythm (your body's internal clock) will adjust to the new routine, and you'll start to sleep better. Also, wake up at your regular time, even if you feel groggy.

Make sure your room is at a comfortable temperature and that your bedding and bed are comfortable.

Stop using your phone and other screens about an hour before bedtime. Screens emit blue rays that disrupt our circadian rhythms and disrupt your sleep cycle.

Avoid super-active and energetic activities about 2 hours before bedtime. Physical activities that excite you and raise your heart rate, such as scrolling rapidly through social media, increase your levels of adrenaline (a hormone your body produces that excites you and can also increase stress). With a surge of adrenaline in your body, you are likely to have trouble getting to sleep on time.

Second, start eating healthy. If you have a lot of packaged, processed junk foods in your diet, this could be the reason for various health problems you experience, such as lethargy, exhaustion, or diabetes.

In addition, such foods contain tons of harmful chemicals, GMOs (genetically modified organisms), artificial sugars, and trans fats that can disrupt your hormones, cause mood swings, and increase your chances of developing serious health conditions.

Slowly replace these foods with healthy options such as leafy greens and other vegetables, fruits, lean meats, soy products, beans, legumes, organic dairy products, and nuts.

At the same time, focus on staying hydrated throughout the day. You should drink 2 to 3 liters of pure water every day. If it is difficult to drink enough plain water, try fresh juices, smoothies, herbal teas, and water.

Also, start getting more active. Some form of physical activity should be part of your daily routine, even if it is just 10 minutes. You can do yoga, Pilates, kickboxing, swimming, exercise, dancing, jogging, walking, or running. The idea is to engage in vigorous physical activity that gets your heart rate up and your muscles working.

Start small with 5 minutes a day and slowly increase the amount of time you spend exercising. Ideally, you should reach 30 to 40 minutes in about 3 to 4 months.

Look for ways to stay active and walk more throughout the day. Take the stairs instead of the elevator. Do chores such as picking up food from the kitchen yourself instead of asking someone else; instead of ordering groceries, walk to the store if it is nearby.

As you work on all these practices, think as positively as you can. Keep telling yourself that you are healthy and happy as you work on these guidelines. Also, try to keep a journal of your daily activities and note your performance to keep track.

How to Create Physical Wealth (Financial Wealth)

Creating financial wealth is easier than you think. You'll make more money with just a few measures, tips and tricks.

But just to satisfy your hunger, here are some key tips for creating more financial wealth.

Always be clear about how much money you want from your job, business, or financial endeavor. The clearer you are, the easier it will be to work toward your goal and harness the power of the LOA.

Put your best effort into your job and any activity you are involved in, whether it promises a financial outcome or not. Hard work combined with sincerity always pays off. Even if you volunteer for an activity with no financial return, your dedication to the task will bring you prosperity and happiness. Also, this effort often leads to financial income from another activity.

Let me tell you a story to show you what I mean. Many years ago, I was working on a food drive for a charitable organization around Christmas. It took 6 to 7 hours of my time each day. I enjoyed working on this drive and gave it my best effort. Those were the days when financial prosperity was far from my mind. Just one week later, I was offered a great job opportunity by one of the other volunteers on that drive, who was also a very wealthy and successful businessman.

Keep track of the money coming into and going out of your account and your life. Write down your income, salary, or earnings from your business or freelance ventures. Also write down your expenses. This is a helpful strategy for keeping track of your income and expenses. It also helps you identify areas and activities you can cut back on to manage and control your spending.

Set a weekly "savings" amount and set it aside each week. You can start with $10 or $20 a week and increase the amount every few weeks. For example, after saving $10 a week for about 4 weeks, you can double the amount to $20 a week.

Find a profitable and viable income and investment stream to invest and grow your savings. For example, if a friend runs a successful Amazon affiliate blog, you can invest in his project or start one of your own.

These are a few tips I wanted you to start thinking about and working on. Keep reading, because this gem of a book is full of tips and strategies that will increase your wealth.

How to Nurture Emotional Wealth
Emotional wealth is about understanding, exploring, embracing and working with emotions.

Here are some helpful ways to cultivate emotional wealth.

Start by spending just 5 to 10 minutes each day with yourself. Sit quietly wherever you can find some peace, and think about some of your most intense emotions and those you experience frequently. It is better to have a journal and pencil with you so that you can write down your thoughts.

Each of us has certain emotions that we experience frequently and that affect our thinking and decision-making. For example, years ago, anger was an emotion that I felt quite deeply and regularly. I used to lose my cool over trivial things like not finding my keys, being late for work because I slept late, not having hot enough water to take a shower, etc.

When I started working on building emotional wealth, I realized that anger was like my second name and I was giving it too much power over me.

Likewise, dedicate some of your daily time to digging into the emotions you feel are controlling you. The best way to do this is to write down the emotions you feel frequently and strongly, and then explore them one by one.

Consider how a particular emotion affects you and how it has affected your life in the past, and continues to do so in the present.

Also consider how a particular emotion makes you behave in different situations. Write down the instances in which the emotion has made you behave in a certain way and the effect it has had on your life.

Also consider whether you are reacting or responding to an emotion. Reacting to something means giving in to the impulsive thought that comes into your mind when something happens. Someone says something mean to you that makes you want to react with verbal outrage. If you react with hostility towards that person, that will be your default reaction.

But you can change this behavior, when you take a short time-out from a certain situation that has overwhelmed you or affected you in a certain way. Then you think about it, you think about the best way to move forward, and you take that action.

Sometimes, even when you are responding to something, you may need to take a rather drastic action, but if you have thought it through and feel it is necessary, go with it. For example, you may need to end a business partnership with someone because of their dishonesty. Ending a partnership may seem drastic, but it is probably the right thing to do if you feel it is not serving you well.

Going back to understanding your emotions, consider how they have affected your life and finances if you feel you are over-reacting. Perhaps you lose motivation easily, and you've had many different career paths, which may be why you haven't grown financially.

Once you have a better understanding of how a particular emotion affects you and how to deal with it, it is time to learn the basics of building emotional wealth. First, you must learn to sit with your emotions every day. Each day, just sit quietly alone and observe your emotions and think about different things that have happened during the day or in the past. For example, if you had a bad day at work and are feeling upset, sit with your frustration and sadness.

Then take a few deep breaths, inhaling through your nose and exhaling through your mouth.

After a few minutes of doing this, you will probably feel calmer. Now think about how you want to handle this emotion. If you are upset, how can you feel better? You will probably come up with some ideas. Write them down. For example, in this case, you might think of watching something funny, talking to a good friend, eating something delicious, or going for a walk.

Go through this list and try anything that seems to work for you. For example, taking that long walk. Make sure you do it right away. If you cannot do it right away, do something else. When you are doing this activity, focus only on the moment.

As you walk, notice the buildings you pass, the trees you see, and how being outdoors makes you feel. The goal is to distract yourself from the upsetting or overwhelming emotion you just felt.

Then think about that emotion again. It is likely to be less intense now. Now is a good time to think about how to respond to it. So, if you were feeling sad and discouraged before, think about your feelings now and why they are the way they are. If you feel depressed because no one at work appreciates you, think about how you can get the appreciation you need. A top answer would be to improve your performance and your behavior toward others. Start doing that and the sad feeling will soon disappear.

Whenever you sit with your emotions, think about the reaction you gave or would have given and how that will affect you. Think about how you can respond to that emotion. If someone insults you, would you rather insult them or look them straight in the eye and ask them if they are okay? The latter is a powerful psychological tip to thwart insulting behavior and make the other person realize their mistake.

Also, be aware of how different emotions manifest in your behavior. For example, if you lock yourself in your room and don't see anyone for days when you're sad, that's how your sadness manifests. If you sing out loud when you're happy, that's a manifestation of your happiness. The more you begin to observe the manifestations of your emotions, the better you will understand them.

Whenever you feel a particularly intense emotion that overwhelms you, observe it and accept it. At that time, speak kindly to yourself and ask the emotion what it is trying to tell you. For example, if you are envying someone, ask your envy, "What are you trying to tell me," or, "why are you here?"

You will probably get surprising answers such as, "I feel that no one sees me" or "I am not enough." Think of positive responses to such answers. Say kind things to yourself such as 'I am enough for me,' 'This too shall pass,' or 'I am fine and will feel even better in time.' Trust me, being kind to yourself works like magic, so try it as much as you can.

Now, whenever you feel an intense emotion erupt within you, sit with it, think about it, embrace it, and then decide how to respond to it. It will take some time to get the hang of this practice, but soon you will master it. During this time, you may make a few mistakes. When you should be quiet, you may blurt out something rude to the other person when you are angry.

When such slip-ups happen, be kind to yourself, forgive yourself for the mistake, ask the other person for forgiveness if you have wronged someone, and then try to behave better the next time. Hopefully, after a few tries, you won't make the same mistakes.

With time and practice, you will begin to cultivate emotional wealth. You will also find it easier to manage your emotions and cultivate a positive attitude that allows you to move forward gracefully. A big plus of building emotional wealth is that it will do wonders for your relationships, allowing you to bond better with loved ones and form cordial and lasting professional relationships.

How to Cultivate Intellectual Wealth

To cultivate spiritual wealth, here are some proven tactics you can try:

First, pay attention to your work and do it with attention and dedication. The more you immerse yourself in your work, the better you will become at it, which will help you hone the skills you need.

At the same time, you will discover your shortcomings and the areas in which you need to improve. For example, if you are a graphic designer but your designs are repetitive, you need to unleash your creative power. If you are a teacher and you teach fifth grade, but you often get feedback that your students are not understanding the various concepts you are teaching, you probably need to work on that.

Look for different courses, programs, techniques, and ways to improve in the area where you are currently lacking. Continuing with the example of lacking creativity as a graphic designer, you can find a good design course online and enroll in it. You can also research different innovative designers and their work and try to learn from them.

Make sure you practice what you learn and try to improve, because the old saying "practice makes perfect" is true.

As you do this, think about and research what other skills you need to develop to improve your work. Take small steps towards constant and continuous growth, and soon you will be leading the way.

You need to think about the things you want to do in the future to achieve your financial goals, and the specific skills you need to achieve them. If you are thinking of learning to code to create your app, start by taking coding classes online. There are both free and paid options available, so choose one that suits you best, or you can mix the two.

Also, observe life, people, experiences, and things. See how different people behave in different situations. Observing people is an art that teaches you a lot about human emotions and psychology. It also improves your intellectual abilities and helps you react better in dynamic situations.

Another thing you need to work on is developing a reading habit. Read books, articles, blogs, and papers on a variety of topics. From science to health to gardening to politics to business to entertainment to sports to lifestyle to psychology— read as much as you can.

The more you read, the more you broaden your horizons, and your ability to accept different things and adapt to different situations. You will also learn more about the world and raise your IQ. Start by reading about a topic that interests you the most to build a reading habit. Start by reading just a few pages per day.

You can also get audiobooks and listen to them while traveling, or doing routine chores such as cleaning or cooking. When used wisely, multitasking is a good tool, but avoid it when doing important things. Over time, start reading about different topics.

These tips may seem like a lot to digest, so take it slow. Start with the first step and slowly add more practice to your routine.

How to Nurture Social Wealth

The more you work on creating emotional and intellectual wealth, the better your interpersonal relationships will become. That's because understanding your emotions allows you to be kinder and more respectful to others.

And when you become intellectually wealthy, you learn better ways to interact with people, find it easier to start conversations, and understand human psychology. As a result, all this knowledge improves your relationships.

Here are several strategies for cultivating social wealth:
Always greet everyone warmly, be it your family, friends, co-workers, neighbors, or people you pass on the street. Greeting people warmly helps build a good rapport with them and makes you seem like a nice, warm person.

Ask people how they are feeling and how their day went. Also, if you are close to someone, ask them questions about their personal life so they know you are interested in hearing what they have to say.

When someone is talking to you, maintain direct eye contact with short pauses so you don't come across as a creepy person. Direct eye contact makes others feel that you are listening to them.

Avoid interrupting others when they are talking to you, whether it is your partner, children, friends or colleagues. Interrupting breaks the flow of the conversation and also comes across as rude. The more you listen to others, the more they will open up to you, which builds trust between you and the other person. Trust is a very valuable emotion to cultivate because it strengthens your relationship with others. Also, when others begin to trust you, they listen to you, which makes you feel valued.

Compliment your loved ones and even people you work with, including your boss. Say nice things like, "I like your shoes," "You look beautiful today," "You have a nice smile," "I love how honest you are," and things like that. Praising people makes them feel good about themselves and brings them closer to you.

Try expressing your feelings to your loved ones to strengthen your bond. Tell your partner how much you love them and how much they mean to you. Let your children know that you are proud of them and appreciate them. Similarly, occasionally say loving things to your friends, parents, siblings, co-workers, etc.

Whenever possible, give gifts to the people you care about. Giving gifts on birthdays, anniversaries, holidays, and special occasions is great, but you can do it anytime. Giving does not mean buying an expensive pearl necklace for your wife or a $200 Lego set for your kids.

Little things like a piece of candy, a flower, a love note, or a candle can mean a lot when given with love. You can also get useful things for your loved ones. If you know a friend is moving and may not be able to cook the day she moves, make her dinner and give it to her.

Whenever someone opens up about their feelings and shares something private with you, listen respectfully. It is okay if you disagree; still respect and listen without judgment. Be accepting of others in order to understand them better and bring them closer to you.

Try to socialize with like-minded and different people. Attend seminars, workshops, reading groups, and social gatherings to expand your social circle. You will also make new friends and contacts who can be helpful at different times.

Look for different online groups you can join to interact with people globally and even locally. You do not have to be friends with everyone, but knowing more people will increase your social exposure and improve your social wealth.

Start by being nice to the people in your social circle and your loved ones, and slowly work on expanding your networks. It will take some time, but if you stick to the above practices, you will soon be overflowing with social wealth.

How to Nurture Spiritual Wealth

When you are spiritually wealthy, you can build a very healthy and satisfying life. Here's what you need to start cultivating spiritual wealth.

In addition to 5-minute sessions to explore and understand your emotions and behaviors, set aside ten minutes each day to explore yourself and your purpose in life. It can be any time of day when you don't have anything urgent to attend to and can quietly focus on yourself. You can even set an alarm to remind you of this task.

During this time, sit comfortably in a quiet room with your journal and write down your thoughts. You can record yourself talking about these things if writing long notes does not work.

Now think about what you want to do with your life. Ask yourself questions such as, "What am I meant to do? What brings me joy? What excites me? What will make me feel fulfilled and happy? What value can I add to the world?"

Take your time and think deeply about each question. Write down all the answers you get and try to make a connection between them.

Another thing you need to do is to focus on the connection between the skills you have acquired so far, your passion (something that never bores you), your talent, and the value you want to add to the universe. So far, the skills you have acquired come from any job or the various tasks you have done professionally.

For example, if you are an accountant, you must have acquired some skills. These skills are your assets. Now, your passion may be to teach, your talent may be your confidence, and maybe you want to teach people more about accounting. If you combine all of these, your goal may be to provide others with more knowledge about accounting so that they can seamlessly manage their personal and professional accounts, avoid making mistakes, and avoid getting caught in scams.

Similarly, you need to explore different dimensions of yourself and look for the hidden connection between them. This latent connection will bring you closer to your life's purpose.

Also, read various books on spirituality and on the lives of successful people who have found their purpose. Read the biographies of Sam Walton, Jack Ma, Warren Buffett, and other thought leaders. Reading books provides knowledge that helps you think clearly and increases your spiritual wealth.

These small tasks may seem boring and overwhelming, but I encourage you to start working on them. You'll be amazed at how much you will begin to know and enjoy once you peacefully know the "real" you.

How to Nurture Psychological Wealth

In order to cultivate psychological wealth, you must begin to work on attaining all the other types of wealth discussed above. Psychological wealth revolves around your sense of fulfillment and contentment that comes when you begin to live a healthy life.

When you have social wealth, you find love and joy in the world. With physical (health) wealth, you can live a healthy life. Emotional wealth gives you better control over your emotions and thoughts so that you can manage them wisely. Intellectual wealth helps you become more skilled, knowledgeable and assertive. Spiritual wealth enables you to live a meaningful life and direct all your activities in the right direction. Financial wealth gives you the means to do things with more freedom.

Of course, when you acquire even a little bit of all these different kinds of wealth, you begin to find balance in your life and improve your psychological wealth.

So, I suggest that you start working on all these types of wealth, one by one, and your psychological wealth will automatically improve.

Balancing material (and non-material) aspects of wealth

A sense of balance brings a lot of serenity and contentment. As human beings, we all want a state of balance in everything we do. This includes the various dimensions of wealth.

Balancing the material and non-material aspects of wealth is crucial to making your life healthy and prosperous.

Here's what you can do to achieve this: First, understand that what is destined for you will come to you, so be patient and focus on thinking positively. Running after things and chasing money makes you seem greedy and sends mixed messages to the universe. Your focus needs to be more on adding value to the world. The more you do that, the more abundant you will become.

Second, begin to be grateful for what you have. There's a whole chapter dedicated to gratitude, and reading it will enlighten you more about the wealth of gratitude. Understand that when you are grateful, you are sending happy thoughts to the universe. The universe then sends you more of the good things.

In addition, gratitude brings a sense of contentment that shifts your focus from what you don't have to the many blessings in your life - and yes, there are many. So be more aware of your blessings and be grateful for them every day.

Third, know your basic and most important expenses and work smart and hard to meet them. If you somehow meet your basic expenses, be grateful and appreciate your efforts. Meanwhile, keep striving to fulfill your purpose in life. As you get closer to it, money will flow in.

Also, try to be nice and kind to those around you, even strangers. Find ways to help others. You could help someone carry their bags in the grocery store, help an elderly person cross the street, ask a friend if they need help moving into a new place, and do as many of these little things as you can. These gestures bring more empathy and generosity into your attitude, and bring a sense of harmony into your life.

Set monthly milestones for all the different types of wealth you have learned about. As you begin to achieve these milestones, you will feel a sense of accomplishment that will help you balance the material and non-material aspects of wealth.

If you have the means to indulge in something luxurious or something you have always wanted, go for it. For example, if you have been meaning to go on a vacation with your partner, and now have some funds to finance a weekend getaway, go and have some fun.

If you wanted to buy a new laptop and you can afford it, buy it. Don't overspend when money is tight, but if certain purchases or expenses are possible, it doesn't hurt to indulge. Doing things for yourself and fulfilling your desires makes you feel that your life is about you and brings harmony.

Finally, slowly work on improving your complaining attitude. When things go wrong, think about what you learned from the experience and all the positive little things. For example, if you failed to close a deal, think about how the experience taught you what mistakes not to make next time.

If you missed a job opportunity because you had to take care of your sick mother, focus on how the experience gave you time to bond with your mother. Thinking about the positive aspects of an experience brings more gratitude and alleviates any miserable feelings you may be struggling with. It also helps you to have a more optimistic outlook, which is crucial to creating wealth.

So, that's how you can balance the different aspects of wealth. And as you work on achieving this sense of balance in your life, your psychological wealth begins to grow with powerful momentum.

Now, let us move on to the next chapter to understand the scarcity mindset that is important to becoming wealthier.

"Working because you want to, not because you have to, is financial freedom."

—**Tony Robbins,** motivational speaker and bestselling author of *Awaken the Giant Within*

Chapter 4:
Breaking Down the Myth
of Scarcity

*'Your scarcity mindset is keeping you poor despite your hard work.' — **Anonymous***

If you are where you were a few years ago in terms of financial wealth, you are getting poorer every day. One of the reasons contributing to this state of affairs is a **scarcity mindset**.

But what is a scarcity mindset, and how does it affect your ability to create and grow wealth? In this chapter, we will find out.

The Scarcity Mindset

Scarcity refers to not having enough of something, or not having what you need. A mindset is a set of opinions, beliefs, and ideologies. Taken together, a scarcity mindset refers to a thought process that makes you focus on things you don't have. This mindset comes with an underlying belief that you will never have what you want.

Such a mindset can make you feel unsatisfied and that things will never be enough. Nothing seems good enough, and despite the happy times, you somehow find something to be upset about. You may always be afraid that what you have will slip through your fingers. Therefore, you will have a habit of hoarding things, be it time, love, or money. If you're afraid that giving things away is bad because you'll have nothing left, you're probably a hoarder and have a scarcity mindset.

The thing about a scarcity mindset is that it is not just about limiting your thoughts about money. It is an all-encompassing approach that applies to different things for different people.

But how do you know if you have a scarcity mindset? Here are some statements you are likely to say when you have a scarcity mindset:

- *I'll never have enough money.*
- *I can never own a house.*
- *I will always be single.*
- *'No one will ever love me.*
- *I will never have the success I want.*
- *No matter how hard I try, I can never lose the weight.*
- *I keep missing out on great opportunities in life.*

Yes, it is normal to have such thoughts from time to time. I mean, we go through hard times that can affect us negatively. If you think about scarcity often, you start to cultivate a scarcity mindset.

Let us evaluate the cause of such a mindset, because we can solve it once we identify its source.

Historical and Psychological Roots of the Scarcity Mindset

The scarcity mindset is not a new concept. It has been a fact of what we call the "human experience" for as long as humans have existed. As humans evolved, materialism, wealth and poverty came into play. These factors also played a role in reinforcing the scarcity mindset.

Scarcity Thinking Evolved with the Early Humans The story of how a scarcity mindset came into our lives begins with the story of the human race.

Thousands of years ago, when man first came into the world, things were not as easy as they are today. Those were the times when people had to fight hard to survive. They had to fight enemies like the Wooly mammoth and the saber-toothed tiger. Natural disasters like floods, famines, and avalanches were always ready to bombard them because we had not developed sophisticated ways to deal with these disasters.

There was always the fear of not surviving. Even though things improved as man evolved and learned to fight these problems by creating tools, fighting mechanisms, and various other aids, the fear remained.

In one way or another, this fear of not being able to survive and not having enough gave rise to the scarcity mentality. Human beings had a lot to go through at that time, which explains why they began to fear the loss of things and the fear of survival.

This fear and insecurity continued with human beings as we evolved over time. With time, mankind evolved. People began to study different subjects and concepts. We discovered new theories and created new inventions. Soon, technology and media came into play.

With all these developments came the competition to be better. People wanted to be better than before and have access to more resources, comfort, and luxury. While competition can be healthy, it can also teach us fear. When we strive for more, we also fear losing what we have; either way, this fear reinforces our scarcity mindset.

In addition, modern media portrays people with more money as successful. If you see a person in an advertisement driving a beautiful Mercedes and you do not have a luxurious car, you are likely to feel insecure.

In addition, many companies and brands capitalize on people's fears. Phrases and words like 'before it gets too late', 'before the stock runs out', 'limited time opportunity' and the like are common in the media. These words affect human psychology. In one way or another, they compel people to take the desired action. The fear of missing an opportunity or not getting what they want reinforces their scarcity mindset.

That's how the scarcity mindset has grown psychologically over time.

Impact of Scarcity Mindset on Personal and Financial Growth

Unfortunately, the scarcity mindset does nothing positive for your personal, emotional, spiritual and financial growth. All it does is weigh you down.

Imagine carrying a sack of cotton and walking down a long road. It does not feel heavy because cotton is quite light. As you walk down the road, you come across a large puddle of water.

Suppose you accidentally slip and the bag absorbs all the water. When you carry the soaked cotton bag, it now feels heavier than before. You know that you have to carry it to carry its weight. It feels uncomfortable, but you keep moving. Lost in your thoughts, you don't see a rock in the path and trip over it. The sack falls off your back and lands in a pond.

You are obviously upset, but you get up anyway. You pull the bag out of the pond and roll it over your back. Your back is now carrying the water-soaked cotton, which is much heavier than it was before. It strains your back as you move it. With every step you take, your back and legs begin to kill you.

Imagine your thought process during this time. Chances are it will be negative. Thoughts like, "Why did this have to happen to me?", "What good is this cotton?", "Why is my life so bad?" and the like are likely to be circling your mind.

Along with these worries, you're also worried about the ruined cotton, and that's when scarcity thoughts come in. What will I sell now? The cotton is ruined, and so are my chances of selling it and making some money?' 'How will I survive this week?' and similar thoughts disturb you.

The sack of cotton represents your mindset. As you face certain obstacles, the sack becomes heavier. As it continues to weigh you down, it brings negative and scarcity-centered thoughts that reinforces your scarcity mindset.

This is what happens when you have a scarcity mindset. It becomes contaminated with every problem you encounter and clouds your thought process.

A scarcity mindset does not always bring in the negative thoughts I described above, but it does start a stream of scarcity-driven thoughts. Since scarcity thoughts are rooted in fear, that fear also triggers negative thoughts.

Let's break down the effects of a scarcity mindset on your personal and financial growth.

Makes you ungrateful

One of the biggest drawbacks of a scarcity mindset is the lack of gratitude it brings. People who fear losing things may still be grateful for what they have. For example, someone struggling to make ends meet may be grateful for the food on the table, but also fearful of not having enough the next day.

But if you have a scarcity mindset, that fear is so ingrained in your mind that you cannot be deeply grateful for your blessings.

When you are truly grateful for your blessings, you don't focus on what you don't have. You strongly believe that you are blessed and that things will work out for you. Even if you don't believe in a particular faith, you trust the universe to bless you with more.

However, if you have a scarcity mindset, you struggle to have faith in the universe. Feeling that you're not successful or that you don't have enough takes your focus away from your blessings.

Instead of thinking about what you have, you fixate on what you don't have. As a result, you become ungrateful and never take stock of your blessings.

Affects your decision-making ability

A scarcity mindset prevents you from making the best decision for yourself because most of your decisions will be based on fear.

For example, because you feel you don't have enough, you may fear losing what you have. As a result, you don't take risks, try new things and experiment. As a result, you miss out on opportunities.

Hinders career growth

The scarcity mindset also hinders your career growth. You believe that success comes in limited amounts. This means that you only have a few chances to be successful, and if you miss that chance, your success will go to someone else.

You begin to fear losing your opportunities. You are also reluctant to share your knowledge and ideas with others because you feel they are limited. As a result, your coworkers may not like you very much either. If you are reluctant to work with them and bring everyone together as a team, they will be reluctant to work with and support you in the same way.

Whenever an opportunity arises that could help you advance in your career, your superiors would most likely not choose you for it because of your uncooperative attitude.

Negatively affects your relationships

Cultivating a scarcity mentality takes a toll on your relationships. Believing that emotional support, care, love, and respect can be scarce tends to create intense, unhealthy emotions such as jealousy, possessiveness, selfishness, and an inability to celebrate your loved one's successes.

You may feel that your partner does not love you enough, which makes you overly demanding. You may feel that your parents never do enough for you, which can exacerbate your aggression issues.

As a result, you are likely to throw tantrums over small things. It is also possible that you begin to hold back from sharing your feelings with your loved ones, which would only strain your relationships.

The belief that love is a scarce emotion may prevent you from showing affection to your loved ones. When fear takes deep root in your mind, you may be surprised at how strangely you begin to think, feel and behave.

A scarcity mindset only prevents you from bonding well with your loved ones.

It hinders your personal, emotional and spiritual growth.

Feeling that you will never be successful, happy, and secure, and always living in fear of losing things or loved ones, automatically depletes your mental well-being.

You are likely to find it difficult to focus on improving yourself. Because you probably already think that you can never get better. All these negative feelings and thoughts create more mental and emotional stress.

The stress continues to build and eat away at your peace. You are likely to feel an emptiness that grows with time. My intention is not to scare you, but to make you aware of how a scarcity mentality eats away at your well-being.

Effects on Your Financial Growth

If you read the first chapter, remember what I wrote about the traditional view of wealth. If you have not read the previous chapter, I urge you to read the section on *Traditional Beliefs About Wealth*.

All of the beliefs I mentioned are beliefs you are likely to have if you have a scarcity mindset. You probably believe that you can never make enough money.

When you think you can never have enough, you fail to achieve your desired goals. The Law of Attraction (LOA) also has a lot to do with this outcome. According to the Law of Attraction, like attracts like. Whatever you put out into the universe comes back to you.

This means that if you believe that you can never succeed, you will not be able to succeed in the areas you desire. Your thoughts construct your belief system and influence your attitude, behavior and actions. If you believe that you cannot make enough money, your actions will reflect that belief.

Also, the thoughts we have travel out into the universe. Now, everything in this universe carries a certain energy and aura. As our thoughts travel, they attract their thoughts, ideas and beliefs of the same or similar energy.

Your scarcity thoughts, focused on not being able to make enough money, attract similar thoughts and ideas to you. Now these thoughts are connected to different people and therefore different experiences. As a result, you attract people, ideas and experiences that do not support you in making enough money.

But you can improve your scarcity mindset. As much as you think you cannot do better or let go of such thoughts, you absolutely can.

Strategies for Recognizing Scarcity Thoughts

To become wealthy, you must improve your mindset by shifting from a scarcity to an abundant mindset. The first step is to recognize your scarcity thoughts and then slowly break them.

Once you have identified and worked on your scarcity-driven thoughts and beliefs, you must shift to an abundance mindset.

So how do you identify these thoughts? Recognizing scarcity thoughts is not that difficult. However, because you have been cultivating a scarcity mindset for some time, it has become deeply ingrained in your system. As a result, you have difficulty recognizing such thoughts and beliefs.

But the good news is that this book provides helpful strategies and approaches that give you a deeper understanding of the psychology of the scarcity mindset. Once you understand how scarcity thoughts develop, you can easily identify them.

Notice When You Have Tunnel Vision

One of the biggest drawbacks of the scarcity mentality is that it creates 'tunnel vision.' When you have tunnel vision, you allow scarcity-based thoughts to control you, and you struggle to recognize them in time.

To recognize your scarcity thoughts, you must first recognize when you have tunnel vision. So let us first give you an understanding of tunnel vision and what it does.

Understanding Tunnel Vision

Imagine that you are wearing blinders like a racehorse. With the blinders on, you can see everything in front of you and nothing on the horizon.

This phenomenon is called "tunnel vision," and it causes you to focus only on what you can see or experience, and not on the bigger picture. Most of the time, when your scarcity mentality kicks in, you have tunnel vision. That's when you focus completely on your existing problems.

Since you can hear your brain screaming, "Deal with it now or you are dead," you let go of the long-term opportunities.

A good strategy for recognizing and gradually releasing your scarcity mentality is to notice when you get tunnel vision. If you recognize it in time, you need to replace your limiting thoughts.

Recognizing Tunnel Vision

Here's what you need to do: Keep track of your thoughts by taking 5-minute breaks every 1 to 2 hours. So, if you have been working on a task for an hour, take a break to check in with your thoughts.

Notice what you are thinking and write it down. You can even record yourself talking about these thoughts.

Next, you need to analyze your thoughts and see if they are fixated only on the problems. For example, let's take a scenario. Your boss has asked you to work with a colleague, and you expect a promotion at the end of the project.

You probably see your colleague as a threat, and feel that if you share your ideas with him, he might beat you to the promotion. If you analyze your thoughts, you will find that you are mainly fixating on the issue that you perceive as a threat.

There is another way to look at this whole situation. You can see it as an opportunity to prove yourself to your boss. You can team up with your colleague and demonstrate your leadership skills by encouraging the person, sharing ideas, and approaching this project as a team effort.

This will make you a bigger and better person, and your boss will likely recognize your efforts and possibly give you a quick promotion.

Whenever you begin to evaluate your thoughts, look for those that focus on tunnel vision.

When you recognize these thoughts, take a few deep breaths. Breathe in through your nose on a count of 4 and out through your mouth on a count of 5 or 6. Taking deep breaths will calm you down and help you focus.

Now you are in a better position to think clearly. Think about whether there is a bigger picture of the matter at hand. In the example above, the bigger picture is acting maturely and getting the promotion by letting go of your scarcity thoughts.

If you can see even a tiny glimpse of the bigger picture, write it down. Think about it for a few minutes, and you will be able to calm your scarcity-driven thoughts.

Try this exercise a few times a day with different scarcity-based thoughts, and slowly you will overcome them.

Recognize your fear

One of the biggest causes and triggers of scarcity-centered thoughts is fear. In most cases, scarcity stems from the fear of losing things, not having enough, and not getting better.

To recognize scarcity thoughts, you must recognize and understand your fear. Your fear can manifest in many ways. Sometimes it comes as a paralyzing thought that prevents you from thinking clearly. At other times it can cause analysis paralysis.

Analysis paralysis is when you find it difficult to analyze a situation and make a decision. When you are afraid to lose something, experiment, or try something because you are afraid of failing, you can find yourself in a quandary where you struggle to put your foot down. You don't know what to do because everything seems confusing and stressful.

Neither of these scenarios is fruitful for you. You must develop the ability to understand and recognize your fear. Once you begin to recognize it, you'll know when it hits you and how it weaves various paralyzing and scarcity thoughts in your mind. Then you'll begin to recognize those thoughts as well.

Here's how you can achieve this goal:

I have taught you to take short "self-reflection" or "checking in with your thoughts" breaks.

During these breaks, analyze your thoughts, feelings, and behaviors. See if there are any signs of fear in your behavior or thoughts. For example, if you come across an investment opportunity and find yourself looking for someone to lend you a loan when you are already in debt, your fear is controlling your behavior.

If you notice fear in your behavior, calm it down. Taking deep breaths is a good idea. You can also take a short walk down the street, drink a warm or cool (whatever works for you) beverage, or just shake your body a little. You need to distract your mind from the emotion of 'fear'.

Once you are somewhat distracted, visualize that fear as a color or shape. Now ask your fear, 'What are you trying to tell me?

Write down the answer you receive. Perhaps your fear is trying to tell you that you may not get another good investment opportunity.

Now you need to have a conversation with your fear and help it understand that decisions made from a place of fear rarely prove fruitful. This is a dialog that will take some time, so be patient with yourself. If your fear tells you, "You only have this one chance to make money," you can respond with something like, "I will get many more chances if I keep trying.

Your fear is likely to throw scarcity-based arguments at you. You must remain calm and respond logically. It will take some time, but soon you will be able to move out of this position of fear.

Similarly, if you are struggling to make a decision, focus on the primary emotion you are experiencing. Ask yourself questions like, "What am I feeling? Am I afraid of losing something?' 'Why can't I make a decision?' and the like.

Write down the answers you get and reflect on them.

Now converse with your fear as I taught you above. Try to present it with logical arguments; soon it will calm down.

Make sure that this is not a one-time practice. You need to have conversations with your fears and scarcity mindset several times a day. The more you think about and analyze these things, the better you will be able to break these thought patterns.

Accepting Your Scarcity Mindset and Building the Intention to Change It

As you begin to recognize your scarcity-centered thoughts, you must accept that you have a problem that needs to be addressed. Remember, no problem ever solves itself if you don't accept that it exists. To work on your scarcity mindset, you must accept it and build an unwavering intention to improve.

Begin to observe your thoughts as much as possible each day.

Every time you think about your career, your goals, your success, or about money, write down your thoughts.

If you notice any hints of fear and insecurity, you are likely to have a scarcity mindset.

Now you need to analyze how this mindset has held you back. Maybe you have missed some good growth opportunities because of it, or maybe you have never experimented and done things you wanted to do. Maybe you wanted to be a songwriter, but did not experiment with it because you were afraid of losing your current job, which was paying your bills at the time.

Even though you are still earning, you are dissatisfied with your income and lack fulfillment. Perhaps if you hadn't been so afraid, you would have been in a better position regarding your career and finances.

By examining your thoughts and your life in this way, you can better understand your scarcity mindset and how it has been holding you back.

Now you need to make an intention to work on it. It must be a positive statement that describes your intention to work on the issue and defines why you want to address this goal. Having a reason is important because it solidifies your commitment and helps you return to your goal when your motivation wanes. So, your intention might be something like, "I am going to work on improving my scarcity mentality in order to live a free, happy, and balanced life.

Say this statement loudly, clearly and determinedly at least ten times. Say it like you mean it. It will sink in after the fourth or fifth repetition. You will probably notice changes in your emotions, feelings, and expressions. You will feel more motivated to improve your scarcity mindset because you now believe it is possible and that doing so will improve the quality of your life.

Wake up each day, review your intention, and write it down. Speak it out loud as you write it down. The more you practice, the better it will become engrained in your mind and slowly take over your scarcity mindset.

Transition to Building an Abundance Mindset

Your goal is to develop an abundance mindset. As you recognize and overcome your scarcity mindset, you gradually move toward an abundance mindset, which is the opposite of a scarcity mindset.

An abundance mentality is free of fear and jealousy. It makes you believe that success is unlimited. Your success isn't dependent on the success of others, and you will get bigger and better if you keep trying and cultivate gratitude, positivity and generosity. Instead of hoarding things and emotions, you give back to people.

I will discuss the abundance mindset later, so bear with me. So far, you know the basics of building an abundance mindset and how to recognize your scarcity mindset.

Let us go one step further and help you understand the more positive counterpart to the scarcity mindset: the abundance mindset.

"Your economic security does not lie in your job; it lies in your own power to produce—to think, to learn, to create, to adapt. That's true financial independence. It's not having wealth; it's having the power to produce wealth."

—**Stephen Covey, bestselling author of** *The 7 Habits of Highly Effective People*

Chapter 5:
The Power of an
Abundance Mindset

'Abundance is a mindset. When you believe in the limitless possibilities of the universe, you open yourself up to receiving abundance in all areas of your life.'

Abundance is when things are abundant, and an abundance mindset focuses on that very thought. To be truly wealthy, you must cultivate an abundance mindset and slowly move away from a scarcity mindset.

Let's talk more about an abundance mindset so you can better understand it, followed by tips and strategies for developing it.

Understanding an Abundance Mindset
Stephen Covey is a renowned author who coined the term "abundance mindset" in his popular bestseller, *The 7 Habits of Highly Effective People*.

According to his findings and those who have studied the abundance mindset in depth, it revolves around the belief that the entire universe is overflowing with resources for everyone. Moreover, there is enough time for everyone to accomplish all their goals.

An abundance mindset is closely related to a growth mindset, which suggests that learning never stops and that there is always room to learn more and opportunities to improve.

Cultivating an abundance mindset makes you believe that nothing is ever limited. There will always be enough resources, opportunities, and time to do what you want.

Unlike the scarcity mindset, the abundance mindset has no sense of fear or insecurity. It frees you and makes you feel free and alive. Of course, when you are not afraid of running out of resources, you become more relaxed and find it easier to work on your goals because you know you can always achieve them.

Those who cultivate an abundance mindset focus on all their blessings and find peace in the present. Instead of worrying about what they don't have, they focus on being grateful and appreciative of what they do have.

This reminds me of a quote from Tony Robbins: "When you are grateful, fear disappears, and abundance appears."

The Characteristics of an Abundance Mindset.
Abundance brings in optimism. You adopt a glass-half-full mentality when you have an abundance mindset. This attitude leads you to find win-win scenarios and pay more attention to your blessings instead of complaining about your half-empty glass.

Abundance focuses on generosity. An abundance mindset makes you believe that there is always enough money, time and resources for everyone to do what they want and need to do. As a result, you become more generous because you no longer fear sharing your knowledge, love, care and resources with others.

Abundance makes you celebrate others and their accomplishments. Because an abundance mindset makes you understand that the world's resources and opportunities will never run out, you know that your good days will come, too. This helps you see the good in people and celebrate their accomplishments and happy moments. You find causes and reasons to be happy, whether they are your own or those of others.

Abundance leads you to experiment and seize opportunities. The belief that there is always more of everything in the world makes you fearless, and you find it easy to try things, see opportunities, and take them.

Abundance makes you focus on becoming the best version of yourself. Fear of losing what you have, and a complaining attitude often turn you into a pessimist. Instead of trying to be better, you complain more. However, when you cultivate an abundance mindset, you understand that there will always be enough for you, and to achieve that, you must improve yourself.

You begin to take time to get to know yourself better and build more self-awareness. You also focus more on your personal growth to become capable enough to achieve and enjoy all that the universe has to offer.

Abundance makes you more mindful of the present. An abundance mindset makes you acknowledge your blessings and brings your focus to the present moment. When you begin to pay attention to what you have, you become more grounded in the present and your mindfulness increases.

As you focus on these qualities, you will find that they are also the benefits of cultivating an abundance mindset.

Adopting an abundance mindset makes you more grateful, happier, mindful, self-aware and generous. It frees you from the fear of not having enough and not being blessed. Instead, it brings a sense of satisfaction and contentment that the universe will always be ready to support you in your endeavors.

The Differences Between the Scarcity and Abundance Mindsets

The most important and striking difference between a scarcity mindset and an abundance mindset is the fear that resources will never run out. A scarcity mindset focuses on the fear that you will never have enough. In contrast, an abundance mindset makes you believe that resources are overflowing, so you will never experience a lack.

This difference then creates more differences between the two mindsets. Those with a scarcity mindset fear losing what they have, so they are reluctant to share their money, time, knowledge, love, care, and other resources.

On the other hand, those with an abundance mindset have complete faith that there is plenty of money, time, love, respect, knowledge, and other resources to share and distribute. As a result, they have a more giving and generous attitude and never shy away from helping those in need.

In addition, the fear of not having enough keeps those with a scarcity mindset from celebrating the success and happiness of others. Those with an abundance mindset are happy to celebrate the accomplishments of those around them because they know that happiness increases when it is shared with others.

Another stark difference between the two mindsets is the absence or presence of gratitude and mindfulness. A scarcity mindset brings in a lot of fear, which often makes you focus on what you have. As a result, you do not acknowledge your blessings enough and become ungrateful. On the other hand, an abundance mindset makes you appreciate what you have.

You are certain that there will always be enough resources for you, so you become more peaceful. This sense of peace helps you become more grounded in the present moment and mindful of your blessings. As a result, you cultivate gratitude and feel happy with what you have.

By now, I'm sure I've convinced you that adopting an abundance mindset is the right way to move forward in life, right? Before we discuss the practical steps to developing an abundance mindset, let's take a quick look at how an abundance mindset influences real-life decisions.

How an Abundance Mindset Influences Real-Life Decisions

Stephen Covey describes the abundance mindset as "flowing from a deep inner sense of personal worth and security. It is the paradigm that there is plenty out there and enough for everyone. It leads to the sharing of decisions, profits, recognition and prestige. It opens up possibilities, options, alternatives and creativity.

When you cultivate an abundance mindset, you can make your life decisions from a mindset of growth, abundance and prosperity. Naturally, your ability to make important and even trivial decisions improves.

An abundance mindset gives you hope that the resources of the universe will never run out and there will always be enough for everyone. This belief brings a sense of calm and peace. You automatically become more positive when you know that you will not lose anything and that you have sufficient resources and opportunities to excel.

This calmness and positivity allows you to think clearly, analyze things in detail, and do your best. When you think from a place of scarcity and fear, you are likely to make rash decisions or get caught up in analysis paralysis and not make any decisions at all. Of course, this affects your productivity and your life in general.

However, an abundance mindset encourages you to think from a place of abundance and comfort. You have faith that things will get better, and you find it easy to think things through and make personal decisions that will lead you to the abundant life you desire and deserve.

In addition, an abundant mindset gives you the courage to have faith in the universe and to experiment with life. When you know that you have nothing to lose and only to gain, you find within yourself the courage to take risks, try new things, step out of your comfort zone, and unlock your true potential. You are not afraid to explore different possibilities, because even if one thing does not work out, another will.

You also become more open and generous with others. Instead of holding back love, knowledge, support and other resources, you share what you have. This attitude helps you attract more good things, because when you send out love, positivity and generosity in the universe, more love and light is returned.

In addition, an abundance mindset positively affects your decisions regarding your personal growth. You understand that the Universe has many resources to offer you, but you must work on yourself to make the best use of them. As a result, you begin to work on overcoming your shortcomings and honing your strengths. When you need to invest in yourself by taking a course or enrolling in a program, you don't hesitate.

As a result, different areas of your life begin to improve, and you find it easy to achieve your goals and live your life with purpose.

Practical Steps for Developing an Abundance Mindset

'Abundance is not something we acquire. It is something we tune into,' said Wayne Dyer.

Tuning into the abundance mindset is what you need to do to attract more abundance your way. So how do you do it?

Here are some practical and actionable strategies for cultivating an abundance mindset.

Examine your limiting beliefs

Limiting beliefs are simply the unconscious beliefs we hold about the world, other people, and ourselves that we allow to keep us from living our lives to the fullest. A good example is if you believe that you don't deserve to be happy, or that you don't deserve to be rich because all of your relatives never made it big in life. If this is the case, you'll find yourself somehow engaging in activities that limit you in order to make your belief system a reality.

Work on Identifying Your Limiting Beliefs

Limiting beliefs are beliefs that keep us from progressing and moving forward. They are usually based on negativity and fear. Such beliefs remind you of your insecurities, failures, and shortcomings and keep you from trying to be better.

For example, if you think you can never be successful or make a lot of money, that's a limiting belief that continues to hold you back. Similarly, if you have a scarcity mindset, you probably have many limiting beliefs that prevent you from trying to move forward in life and attract abundance your way.

One of the most effective ways to develop an abundance mindset is to improve your limiting beliefs and replace them with empowering ones (which I will discuss more in the next step.) To do this, you must first identify and acknowledge your limiting beliefs.

Identifying your limiting beliefs helps you figure out the limiting beliefs that continue to hold you back from all the amazing things your life has to offer. Acknowledging them brings a kind of peace to them. You accept that a problem exists, and instead of running away from it, you embrace it. This is similar to accepting that you have a certain health problem and that you need to work on it instead of avoiding it.

Here's what you need to do to identify and acknowledge your limiting beliefs:

Yes, there is immense power in sitting alone and going through your beliefs. It may seem tedious, but observing your thoughts is the best way to work on yourself and your mindset.

So, take a few minutes each day and observe what kind of beliefs you have. Ask yourself questions such as, "Why am I afraid to try things?", "Why don't I pursue my passion?", "Why can't I get my dream job?", "Why haven't I been able to create the financial wealth I want?

Ask yourself one question at a time and write down the answers you get, one at a time. Your answers will probably reflect your fear and insecurity of failing, not getting what you want, losing things you already have, and the like. For example, if you wanted to start your own business but couldn't, your answer might be, "I'm afraid it won't work," or "If I invest the little money I have, I might lose it. These are your limiting beliefs that you must now understand and accept.

At this point, your only role is to observe and write down your thoughts and beliefs.

Please do this daily. Set alarms to remind you to develop this habit. You can do it at the beginning of the day so you don't forget, and you can do it when you are fresh or even at the end of the day. A great way to start a new habit is to do it right after you wake up so you can work on it right away.

After 5 to 7 days, you will be able to recognize your limiting beliefs while doing routine tasks and chores. Whenever you recognize one of your limiting beliefs, stop whatever you are doing and write it down. If you are cooking, writing, or working on a presentation and you notice limiting beliefs such as "I will not be able to get rich," or "I will not be able to pay my bills this month," or "I will not get this client," simply write them down.

If you are doing something that you cannot stop when a limiting belief comes up, such as driving, talking to a client, meeting with your team, etc., write it down and try to remember it later. It's okay if you miss some limiting beliefs; they will probably come up later and you can write them down then.

Once you have identified and observed your limiting beliefs for about two weeks, you need to acknowledge that they exist and are affecting your life. Sit in a quiet place, take out your journal, and read through the reports of your limiting beliefs.

After reading them, say something about accepting them and making a commitment to work on them. For example, you might say, "I accept that I have certain limiting beliefs that keep me from living a healthy life, so I will now actively work to improve them.

Say this suggestion several times and say it with complete conviction. The more you believe it, the stronger it will become in your mind and help you overcome these limiting beliefs.

Now, whenever you try to observe your limiting beliefs, chant this suggestion first and then evaluate them from a place of kindness. You will find it easier to work with yourself to overcome them.

Once you have identified and accepted your limiting beliefs, you need to move on to the next step: replacing them with more empowering beliefs.

Replace your limiting beliefs with beliefs that empower you

Limiting beliefs are by definition limiting, which means that in one way or another they prevent you from achieving what you want in life and making it better.

These beliefs have kept you from having the career you want, from putting your travel plans on hold, and from staying in situations that never work out for you.

They are just beliefs, not facts.

You know the good thing about that? You can change them.

You can always replace a limiting belief with something better and healthier. That's where empowering beliefs come in.

Empowering beliefs are positive and growth-oriented beliefs that assure you that things will get better and that you can always get better at achieving your desired goals.

Unlike limiting beliefs, empowering beliefs give you faith in yourself and the courage to find your wings, spread them, and soar. For example, instead of telling yourself, "I can never make enough money," tell yourself, "I can make as much money as I want if I dedicate myself to the necessary tasks and achieve my money-related goals.

I want you to do a quick activity right now.

Please write down the empowering statement I wrote above.

Now say it out loud very slowly so that you can concentrate on each word. Also, be loud enough to hear each word ring in your ears. Finally, say it with confidence so that you believe it to be true.

Say it about ten times.

Now, honestly tell me if you feel even the slightest hint of positivity in your mind and begin to believe that you can do whatever you want.

It may take you a few more tries than just 10 to get this effect, so keep trying, and as you hear that yes from within, you will automatically begin to believe that the statement is true.

What happens next is that the statement begins to take root in your subconscious mind. Because you are chanting and writing it every day, your subconscious mind believes that it is important to you, and then it engrains it into your belief system.

Once it becomes part of your belief system, it shapes your attitudes, behaviors, and decisions accordingly. As a result, you find it easier to take action on tasks that help you achieve the goal or improvement of your statement. We call these statements affirmations, which I will discuss later in the book.

Let's focus on the influence of empowering beliefs. This is how they encourage you to work toward self-improvement and your goals.

Now, how can you begin to replace your limiting beliefs with those that are empowering? Here's how:

Take any one limiting belief that has been negatively affecting you and limiting your ability in some way. For example, if your limiting belief is "I always fail at making more money, so it is best not to try," and you feel that it is holding you back from working hard, pursuing your passion, and becoming financially wealthy, you can work on that.

Now you need to change that into an empowering belief by removing the negative and limiting words and replacing them with more empowering and positive words. So, the belief, "I always fail at making more money, so it is best not to try," can become, "I can make more money, and I will sincerely work to attract more financial wealth in my life."

Please write this down a few times. Chanting while writing is an effective way to embed the empowering statement in your mind and slowly turn it into a belief, so try it.

You can even write down this empowering statement and post it on your bedroom wall, bathroom mirror, work desk, and other prominent places in your home and workplace. These reminders will remind you to focus on this statement and incorporate it into your belief system.

Work with this empowering belief for about two weeks until you notice positive improvements in your personality, behavior, and productivity.

Next, work on other limiting beliefs that you want to change, one at a time.

As you work on reframing your limiting beliefs into their empowering counterparts, remember to be kind and patient with yourself.

As you begin to improve your limiting beliefs, you may sometimes find it difficult to hold on to your empowering beliefs and give in to the power of the limiting beliefs. You may procrastinate and not work on your goals, or you may fall back into the trap of a scarcity mindset.

At such times, I want you to be gentle with yourself, go through your empowering beliefs again, re-center yourself, and work to get back on track. If you are consistent in your efforts, magic will soon happen, I assure you.

Keep a Gratitude Journal

At the heart of an abundance mindset is the belief that abundant resources are available.

If you analyze this belief, you will see that it comes from a place of gratitude. When you are gracious and grateful, you find blessings in everything. This attitude and mindset encourages you to believe that abundant resources and opportunities await you.

Consequently, it helps you develop an abundance mindset. In fact, gratitude is an integral part of an abundance mindset. Therefore, keeping a gratitude journal will help nurture and grow an abundance mindset.

Here's what you need to do: Either get a new journal to record your blessings, or dedicate a section of your existing journal to recording your gratitude.

Start your day by thinking of something you are grateful for. It could be something like "getting a good night's sleep," "living another day," "waking up to a sunny morning during a cold winter," "having food on the table," etc.

Take a moment to reflect on this blessing and write it down in your gratitude journal.

Set alarms for every 3 hours. You can call this 'Gratitude Time.' When you see the reminder for your gratitude time, take a brief 1-minute break and acknowledge one thing for which you are grateful.

It could be a peaceful day at work, your boss appreciating you, eating your favorite lasagna for lunch, no traffic on your way to work, a pleasant conversation with a coworker, or anything else. The idea is to mindfully notice and acknowledge everything that makes you feel happy and blessed. Write this down in your journal/gratitude section.

Now continue to record your blessings every 3 hours. You can even do these gratitude breaks every 2 hours or every hour. I suggest starting with a 3-hour interval to keep things light and easy.

If you cannot write down your blessings as you acknowledge them, write them down at the end of the day. You may forget them when you sit down to make a journal entry. If this happens, do not worry and think of 3 to 5 things you are grateful for during the day. But be sure to write down 3 to 5 blessings each day.

At the end of each week, review all your gratitude entries and you will be amazed at how many things you have to be thankful for. The list will continue to grow each week, and you will continue to feel blessed and thankful.

Gratitude journaling works very well and is a great way to improve your mental health, boost your self-esteem, and strengthen your relationships (both personal and professional). It also helps you attract wealth and abundance your way. Be sure to stick with this practice.

Positively Reframe Your Self-Talk

'Self-talk' refers to how and what you say to yourself. If you observe your thought process in routine life, you may notice how you often ask yourself for suggestions and input whenever you decide or in routine situations. For instance, when getting dressed for work, you may ask yourself, 'What should I wear today?' or when considering applying for a job, you may think, 'Should I apply for it or not?' The answers that you get in exchange for these questions are your self-talk.

Your self-talk affects your thought process, which in turn influences your mindset. You have negative self-talk if you often say demeaning, criticizing, and negative things to yourself. Now, self-talk will automatically affect your ability to develop an abundant mindset.

Imagine every time you think of doing something, talking to someone, or trying a new activity, you hear suggestions like, 'You won't be able to pull it off,' 'You will make a fool of yourself,' 'You won't succeed at it' and the likes. If these suggestions become too much, you start developing negative self-talk. This self-talk usually has a harsh tone, so it will usually respond harshly to most of your questions. In psychological terms, this harsh tone almost always belittling you is also called your 'inner critic.'

One day, you come across a good business opportunity you believe could be very profitable. You want to exercise it and automatically start talking to yourself about it in your head. Since yours is negative self-talk, your inner critic is most likely to pull you down in this case, too. It might bring up your past failures and mistakes and remind you how you have always struggled to pursue a business. It might also remind you of your funds' scarcity, so investing them in a business will be foolish.

The odds are high that your inner critic will succeed in keeping you from doing what you want. Whenever a similar instance occurs, your inner critic is likely to emerge triumphant in weighing you down. Gradually, it teaches you the fear that you won't succeed in your goals because you cannot improve, you will lose resources, and other similar reasons.

As a result, you develop a scarcity mindset in addition to having an inner critic. While this scenario may sound sad, the good news is you can change it for the better by simply working on reframing your self-talk.

If you start talking positively to yourself, you will gradually adopt a positive outlook in all of its areas and domains. As you learn to encourage yourself and become more hopeful, you will also find it easier to build an abundance mindset.

Here's what you need to do: Observe how you talk to yourself in your routine life. Pay attention to the kind of self-talk you have when grocery shopping, going to work, deciding what to wear, writing a post on social media, taking a picture of yourself, interacting with others, cooking, etc.

If you notice yourself saying demeaning, rude, or disrespectful things to yourself, pause there and then.

Take a deep breath and acknowledge that some negative self-talk has happened. You can even say, 'I notice I am talking negatively to myself.'

Now, very gently, reframe that thought to something more positive. So if you said something such as, 'I know nobody will talk to me at the party,' change it to, 'I am sure I'll have a good time at the party, and people will be nice to me.' If you thought, 'I don't think I can pull off this presentation,' rephrase it to, 'I can and will pull off this presentation, and work hard to deliver desired results to my superiors.'

Sometimes, you may not feel like saying such long sentences, so you can simply say things like, 'I can pull it off,' 'The party will be nice,' and 'I can do it.' The idea is to say positive, hopeful, and comforting things to yourself so you move out of the 'fear' zone and into the 'abundance' world.

Whatever you do or think, try to talk positively to yourself at all times.

Positive self-talk will come naturally to you after about two weeks of practicing this. You will also notice a marked improvement in your ability to think in abundance.

Spend Time with People Who Have an Abundance Mindset
'You are the average of the five people you spend the most time with,' said Jim Rohn.

Analyze your personality and then think about the five people you hang out with. You will find that you all have a lot in common. And if there is a scarcity mindset, that may be one of the reasons you are cultivating it.

If you spend a lot of time with certain people, their personality and character traits will rub off on you. Therefore, it is wise to spend more time with positive, growth-oriented people who have an abundance mindset.

Identify the few people in your close social circle with whom you often spend time. They could be your partner, co-workers, children, parents, close friends, siblings, etc.

Now select five people from this list with whom you often talk, listen, share, and spend the most time.

Quietly assess their mindset. A person's mindset reflects his or her behavior, attitude, decisions, suggestions, etc.

Write down the mindset you feel these five people have: scarcity or abundance. If you have trouble identifying a person's mindset, you can write about whether their mindset is more like a scarcity mindset or an abundance mindset.

Next, you need to slowly distance yourself from those with a scarcity mindset and spend more time with those with an abundance mindset. It may not be easy to separate from those close to you, even if they have a scarcity mindset.

For example, if you feel that your spouse has a scarcity mindset, you certainly cannot break up with your significant other (SO) for that reason. But you can talk to your SO about it, gently and slowly, to help your partner develop an abundance mindset.

As for people with a scarcity mindset, you can separate yourself somewhat from neighbors or co-workers, talking to them as needed and not spending long hours with them.

At the same time, find ways to connect more with those who have a nurturing and abundance mindset. Talk to them and ask them about their strategies for staying positive and attracting abundance. The more you spend time with them, the stronger your abundance mindset will become.

Your abundance mindset can do wonders for you, and it is just waiting for you to start working on it. So make a little promise that you will start this journey today. You don't have to do anything big. You can just start by being kinder and more polite to yourself. This will help you build positive self-talk that will shape your abundance mindset.

Developing an abundance mindset is one of the most important steps in attracting wealth and abundance because it helps you gradually unlock your wealth potential.

In the next chapter, we will talk more about unlocking your true wealth potential to become truly wealthy.

"You can only become truly accomplished at something you love. Don't make money your goal. Instead, pursue the things you love doing, and then do them so well that people can't take their eyes off you."

—Maya Angelou, poet

Chapter 6:
Unlock Your Wealth Potential

'The most difficult thing is the decision to act;
the rest is merely tenacity.'
—Amelia Earhart

To be wealthy, you must unlock your wealth potential. Until you do, you will find it difficult to manifest the wealth and abundance you have always dreamed of. Cultivating an abundance mindset and positive thinking are rudiments to attracting the results you desire, but you must also work to achieve your goals.

This is where your wealth potential comes in. What is Wealth Potential?

Your wealth potential refers to your ability to make a certain amount of money in a certain amount of time.

Our unique goals and objectives usually stem from our desires, needs, dreams, and aspirations, and many of them depend on money. To achieve them, we need to use our potential. If it helps us make money, this potential is known as our Wealth Potential.

Your Wealth Potential can include your skills that can be monetized to make money. For example, if you are a life coach and you use this skill to coach people and charge them a certain amount, your skill is your Wealth Potential.

If you have a knack for speaking and think you can hone that potential to monetize it, that also falls under the category of your Wealth Potential.

Your wealth potential includes everything in your personality, attitude and behavior that you can use to achieve your wealth-related goals.

It also requires you to work on your doubts, fears, limiting beliefs, and insecurities. That's important because all of these things keep you from working with complete dedication and hinder your ability to manifest the amount of wealth you desire.

When I say you need to unlock your wealth potential, I mean you need to do what it takes to unleash your ability to achieve your wealth-related goals and manifest the wealth you desire in your life.

Now that you have a clearer idea of your wealth potential, let's talk about how to unlock it.

Identify your assets

Your assets are your strengths, potential, hidden talents and passions. They are your positive attributes, qualities, and interests that you can use to your advantage to unlock your wealth potential.

For example, if you have a good voice and a talent for speaking, this can be one of your strengths that you can use to unlock your wealth potential. Perhaps you can start a podcast on a topic that interests you, such as environmentalism. If this aligns with your life's purpose, you can start podcasting about it, using your good speaking skills. You can create a YouTube channel and work towards monetizing it to start a side hustle and make money.

Let me share with you the steps to identify your strengths and passions.

First, think deeply about your various virtues and qualities. Think about the things that people, especially those who aren't your friends and family, praise you for. People who are not too close to you will usually praise you for something that exists in you, not just to make you feel better.

Their analysis and feedback is usually unbiased, so it is best to focus on that. But yes, good friends and loved ones can also give you unbiased input. So if you have a friend or two who is brutally honest but also loves you dearly, ask them what they think is the most striking quality about you.

For example, if someone thinks you are disciplined, have a good smile, or have a charming personality, you can add those qualities to the list.

You can also write down the qualities you think you have and the qualities that set you apart from others. For example, if you believe that you are honest and that this can help you unlock your wealth potential, write this down in your journal.

Also consider the different subjects, areas and topics that interest you. Knowing your interests and likes will help you create wealth because it will give you an idea of the areas or directions you should pursue. Following your passion or incorporating it into your life is very important.

Your passion is something you rarely get tired of or bored with. It is something you can engage in and enjoy at any time. Incorporating it into your profession or your journey to fulfill your purpose helps tremendously. When you're doing something you love, obstacles don't much dampen your spirit. You may feel stressed at times, but you always find a way to get back on track.

If you are passionate about drawing and your purpose in life is to teach children, you might start an art school, create classes on different dimensions of art to teach this skill, or create videos. Now, if you encounter setbacks along the way, such as not being able to attract clients or not capturing the interest of your audience, you will continue to do what you love.

At the same time, you will also find a way to overcome the problems you are experiencing because of your immense love and interest in this area. So, spend some time exploring your passions and take out the top 5 passions.

We have certain doubts, fears and insecurities that often come into play and hinder our growth. Perhaps you've given in to your self-doubt and personal limitations, which is why you haven't been able to create the wealth you desire.

You must overcome these limitations and insecurities to unlock your full wealth potential. They keep you from believing in yourself, scare you from doing what you want, and remind you of past mistakes that stifle your spirit.

So, let's learn how to break free of these shackles, unleash your true potential, and reclaim your life.

Think of 3 to 5 personal limitations, fears and doubts that have kept you from pursuing your goals and passions. They could be anything, such as People will laugh at me, I'll make a fool of myself, I don't have what it takes to be successful.

You can even go through your limiting beliefs and use them to identify any larger fears and doubts that are blocking your path to success. If your limiting beliefs are also your doubts, use them.

Now you know how to overcome your limiting beliefs and transform them into empowering beliefs. So, practice this exercise regularly.

For any doubts and fears that are different, you need to talk to each doubt and fear to find the root cause. For example, if you fear that "people will laugh at you," why do you think you fear that? Maybe it's because you were laughed at in public once, and it scarred you. Why were you laughed at? What exactly happened? Explore these questions further and you will find out exactly what happened and why.

Understand that the incident is ancient, whether it happened many years ago or a few days ago. Calm yourself by taking a deep breath and saying something comforting to yourself, such as, "It is in the past and I have moved on.

Also, think of something that the incident might have taught you. For example, if you stuttered when people laughed at you, you may know that you need to improve your stuttering. At the same time, you need to understand that people can be insensitive and laugh at anything, so you just need to ignore those instances.

Moving on, think about how far you have come from the instance that somehow gave birth to your fear and self-doubt. You are alive, possibly earning a living and managing your life. All of this deserves applause, so be happy for yourself.

Also, remember to note your small accomplishments every day. If you paid your bills on time, write that down. If you turned in a project on time, write that down. If you had a good talk with your father and your strained relationship with him is improving, write that down.

You need to give yourself credit for these accomplishments. Doing so will comfort you and help silence your self-doubt. As you see yourself doing well in different areas, you'll begin to understand that your doubts are just inner disturbances and not true. Remember, they are only beliefs, not facts; you can change them.

In this way, take 5 to 10 minutes to overcome your self-doubts and limitations. Overcoming your doubts and limitations helps to eliminate the inner issues that keep you from pursuing your goals.

You will also create more space in your mind and life to pursue your purpose, which, as you know, is a great way to experience spiritual abundance and well-being. In addition, you will save the energy that would otherwise be spent worrying about your limitations. You can now use that energy to improve yourself and achieve your goals.

Exercises for Self-Discovery and Skill Development

If you have read this book from chapter one, you have come across many exercises and techniques for self-discovery and skill development. I want to share a few more with you to help you make better progress on this journey to increase your wealth.

Get Out of Your Comfort Zone and Experiment a Little

Often, we create a comfort zone in different areas of our lives and stick to it because it feels easy and comfortable, hence the name 'comfort zone'. This zone keeps us from trying new things, taking risks, and identifying things that we may like or that will be fruitful in the long run.

For example, if you have been a teacher for ten years, that might be your comfort zone. Maybe you don't like your job and you want to do design. But your comfort zone is holding you back.

You must move out of your comfort zone in order to be limitless and attract abundance in abundance. Here's how to do it:

Start by identifying something you want to do. For example, you could take any new skill you want to learn or any passion you want to pursue.

Figure out three ways you can do it. If you want to learn graphic design, you could take an online course, learn from a friend or coworker who is an expert, or take a live class. Find the easiest option and get started.

You can start by spending 5 minutes doing this "new" thing and see how you feel about it.

If you enjoy it or want to continue, increase the time each week.

Also, try doing routine things differently every day. If you drink black coffee, try a latte. When you style your hair, try a different style. When you go to work, take a different route. Little things like these slowly prepare your brain to try new things and move out of your comfort zone. These actions also supercharge your brain cells and improve your ability to think better and act proactively.

Be your superhero/superheroine

I can say with certainty that at some point in our lives, we have all wished for some sort of superpower. We admire superheroes and wish we could be more like them. The truth is, we can. We may have different powers than those shown in the movies and described in the books, but when we unleash them, we can be the best versions of ourselves.

A powerful exercise in self-discovery is to be your superhero. You have to imagine yourself as a superhero doing something incredible. This exercise unlocks your imagination and creativity and often gives you insight into what you want to do.

Here's what you need to do:

Sit in a peaceful place and close your eyes.

Think of a superpower that you can create using your skills, strengths, passions, and abilities. Yes, you must think creatively at this point. Your superpower can be anything from making people love and enjoy math, to helping people be kinder to animals, to running million-dollar businesses and empowering others to do the same. Keep your goals, purpose, strengths, passions and interests in mind and be innovative. Describe them in detail in your journal.

Imagine yourself as a superhero/superheroine with the power you described in the previous step. You can create an imaginary costume and add some effects to your appearance.

When you are ready, imagine yourself using your superpower to do positive things. You could eradicate hunger and poverty, help people learn better, empower them to be confident and speak up, and so on.

Think about this scenario for about 10 minutes, then tune in to your feelings. How are you feeling right now? Write down your feelings and emotions in your journal.

If you do this every day, you will find yourself filled with enthusiasm and optimism about getting closer to your goals. You will also begin to find better ways to create and manifest abundance.

"Money is only a tool. It will take you wherever you wish, but it will not replace you as the driver."

—Ayn Rand

Chapter 7:
Creating Your Wealth Vision and Strategy

*'Strategic planning is worthless -
unless there is first a strategic vision.'*
—John Naisbitt

Once you are in a place where you understand your wealth potential, the next crucial step is to come up with a vision and strategy to create that wealth.

'A vision is not just a picture of what could be. It is an appeal to our better selves, a call to be something more,' said Rosabeth Moss Kanter.

So, what is your vision for wealth creation, and what is your strategy for creating it? Your vision refers to your ability to think about and plan for your future. It is an overall picture of your life, how you want to live, and how you want to shape it.

Let's discuss its importance, its relationship to wealth creation, and strategies for creating your wealth vision.

The Importance of a Clear Wealth Vision

If you have ever talked to successful and wealthy people or watched their stories on video, you must have noticed that almost all of them have a well-thought-out vision for their lives.

Their vision gives them a sense of direction, so they know exactly how to plan their steps. Take the story of Sam Walton, for example. The maestro behind Wal-Mart was very clear about the life he wanted and the business he wanted to build.

His vision was to lower the cost of living for people. He created Wal-Mart stores according to that vision.

Similarly, you must have a vision to live a healthy life with meaning and purpose. Without a vision, we go through the motions every day feeling like we haven't accomplished anything.

Having a wealth-based vision is crucial so that you know exactly what kind of wealth and abundance you are striving for. Your wealth vision helps you in the following ways

It clearly states the type and amount of wealth you want. For example, if you want enough wealth so that you and your loved ones can live comfortably and you can also help those in need, you would have clarity about what you want and what you need to work for.

Without a vision, you may be setting wealth-based goals without connection and alignment. You may work to get a better paying job and then move on to another wealth-centered opportunity. When you keep shifting gears, you confuse yourself and the universe. As a result, you don't get what you want.

Your vision is a comprehensive view of your life. It does not end with the achievement of one or two goals. Instead, it encompasses your entire life and existence. You keep setting meaningful goals and fulfilling your vision. As a result, you stay active and don't become stagnant.

With a clear vision of wealth, you don't lose sight of what you're striving for. Often, when adversity hits us, we become demotivated and sometimes even stop pursuing our goals. When you have a vision, it gives you hope in the midst of darkness. You may stop for a while, but your vision encourages you to get back on track.

Your wealth vision also gives you direction on how to achieve it. Once you know what you want to accomplish, you begin brainstorming ways to make your vision a reality. You identify the steps and activities to achieve your goal and use this knowledge to create a roadmap.

Finally, a wealth vision gives you a deep understanding of your deepest desires and needs. You begin to dig deeper into your thoughts and explore yourself in depth. The more you explore yourself, the more you understand your purpose and mission in life.

With the importance of creating a wealth vision clear, let's move on to the steps for creating a wealth vision and strategy.

Steps to Creating a Personal Wealth Vision and Strategy

Having a clear wealth vision and strategy is critical. These two tools serve as your wealth compass and keep you focused on achieving what you want. Here's what you need to do:

Sit in a quiet place with your journal or recording device. Some of us don't like to write very much. If you are one of them, record yourself talking about your vision on your phone or other recording device.

Take a **few deep breaths and meditate** for a few minutes.

When you feel calm and centered, think about the wealth and abundance you want, what you want to do with it, and how you would use it to add value to those around you.

Close your eyes and think about where you see yourself in the next 20 to 30 years. How wealthy do you see yourself? What kind of wealth do you have? Are you materially rich or do you have a holistic approach to abundance?

Take your time with each question and write down your answers in detail. If you prefer to record your answers, do so. But make sure you have a record of them, so you can reflect on them later and use the information to create a better connection between the different parts. Once you find it, that nexus will lead you to your vision.

Take about 10 minutes each day to reflect on your wealth vision. It is important to go slowly so that you can think deeply about each question and gain deep insight into your vision. Rushing through the process can create a superficial vision that you don't feel connected to.

If you stick to this practice and work consistently, you will have a reasonably clear idea of your vision in about 3 to 4 weeks. It may take you less or more time. We are all different and interpret things in life differently, so respect your individuality and go at your own pace.

Once you have a clear vision, create a strategy to achieve it.

Keep your vision as the end goal. It will most likely take ten or more years. It spans a decade, so you have about ten years to make it happen. What are you going to do in the next ten years to achieve it? You need to think along these lines to develop a plan to manifest your vision.

Now take a moment to think about the basic thing you need to do to accomplish it. For example, if your vision is to be a leading provider of low-cost, high-quality graphic design services that make it easy for people to share their work and better connect with their audiences, the first step would be to learn graphic design if you don't already have that skill.

With that in mind, think about what the next step should be. Create big milestones spread out over a year or two. These would be your short-term goals.

Then think about what you need to do in the next five years. These would be your mid-term goals.

Now take your short-term goal and think about what you need to do to achieve it. Use the first basic step as a benchmark and use it to create monthly plans.

It's best to write everything down so you don't forget or overlook anything important.

If you look at a goal as a whole, it is likely to overwhelm you. Break it down into smaller tasks and weekly milestones to make it more manageable. This strategy gives you something to work on and look forward to each week without feeling overwhelmed.

Make weekly and monthly plans, then start working on the first step. This approach also allows you to create goals and action strategies that align with your vision.

After you have done the above, review everything. If possible, consult with someone you admire, preferably someone you trust, who has achieved similar goals. This person will mentor you and help you further refine your vision strategy.

Make it a habit to review your wealth strategy on a weekly basis. This approach will help you revisit your goals, check that you are actively working on them, and make changes to this strategy.

While you must actively and rigorously work on your action plan, you must also be flexible. Sometimes contingencies come your way unannounced. At those times, you may need to change your course of action. This does not mean that you must abandon your vision and goals. You must find another way to meet the challenge and follow your plan of action.

Record everything, either in writing or verbally. And work daily to achieve your vision. In this pursuit, you are likely to encounter challenges. This is normal and natural.

Change is the only constant in life, so expect things to change over time. This may affect your ability to execute your strategy. But you can also overcome these challenges.

Overcoming Challenges in Executing Your Strategy

Here are some foolproof ways to overcome challenges in executing your strategy:

Review your action plan every night before you go to bed. Strategize for the next day and make a to-do list.

Detail what you need to do, how you will work on it, and what resources you will need. Planning ahead will save you time the next day. It also allows you to prepare for your tasks ahead of time.

Often, we find it difficult to execute a strategy because the necessary resources, such as time and money, are not available. For example, you may plan to make cookie samples for a tasting tomorrow, and just as you are about to bake, you realize that you are short on flour and white chocolate chips. You could go to the grocery store and buy what you need, but that would be a waste of time. Therefore, it is always wise to prepare ahead of time for the next day's tasks.

Figure out your distractions so you can plan a strategy to counteract them in time. Make a list of all the different activities, temptations, and people that might distract you from your work.

If you are tempted to use social media during work hours or are interrupted by uninvited guests in your home office, these are your distractions.

Think of ways to combat them and write them down. You can temporarily block social media or distracting sites, or log out of your social media profiles. As for unplanned visitors, you can set specific meeting times and not entertain them at all costs.

Think about the worst thing that could happen in any situation. That would be your worst-case scenario. Now, for that worst-case scenario, think of some probable solutions. For example, if you plan to pitch your business idea to potential angel investors, the worst thing that could happen would be rejection. If that happens, how do you plan to move forward?

How will you deal with the rejection and with yourself if and when you feel sad? If you plan to do ACCA, what if you don't qualify? Do you have a plan B? Will you stick with your chosen career or switch gears? I understand that thinking about the worst-case scenario can be a bit paralyzing, but thinking about it now will help you strategize a contingency plan in advance.

Also, review your strategy as much as possible. I have discussed this before, but this step is often overlooked. We often don't revisit it after planning and strategizing. Over time, situations often change, presenting us with new threats or opportunities.

If you don't revisit your strategy and make changes accordingly, you may find yourself taking the wrong approach to a problem or failing to capitalize on an opportunity with your old strategy.

One of the biggest challenges you can face in executing your strategy is experiencing financial setbacks. When this happens, you are likely to lose your cool and feel quite discouraged. The right way to fight and handle such setbacks is to build resilience. Resilience is the ability to withstand and recover from difficulties so that you can bounce back and continue doing what you need to do.

I can understand how hard it can sound to endure and recover from a financial setback. However, it is important to build resilience in order to move forward in life. Financially wealthy people are incredibly gritty and resilient. They know that you have to take risks to grow your wealth and be prepared to deal with financial crises.

If you wallow in misery after a setback, you won't be able to bounce back. That's why you need to work on building resilience so that when you face various crises in implementing your wealth vision and strategy, you can handle them successfully.

When you experience a setback, take a deep breath to calm yourself. Once you feel calmer, think about the best way to respond to the situation.

Practice affirmations and visualization to help you imagine yourself getting out of the situation. You'll learn these techniques in the chapters that follow.

Surround yourself with positive people who can lift your spirits during these times.

Keep your eyes on the big picture: your wealth vision, and keep reminding yourself, "This too shall pass. Nothing is permanent and no adversity lasts forever.

Be kind to yourself and forgive your mistakes so you can come up with a solid plan of action to move forward.

Now that you have all the steps outlined, begin to identify your wealth vision and create your strategy. Again, there is no rush to do this right away, but I encourage you not to put it off any longer. The longer you delay, the further away you will be from manifesting your desired wealth. And once you have your vision of wealth, you will find it easy to create value for others.

"Before you speak, listen. Before you write, think. Before you spend, earn. Before you invest, investigate. Before you criticize, wait. Before you pray, forgive. Before you quit, try. Before you retire, save. Before you die, give."

— **William A. Ward**

Chapter 8:
The Role of Value Creation in Wealth Accumulation

'Focus your efforts on adding value rather than on promoting your achievements.'
— Frank Sonnenberg

True wealth creation and accumulation boils down to value creation. If you are committed to becoming holistically wealthy and abundant, you must focus on adding and creating value in the world.

The Concept of Value Creation and Its Relationship to Wealth

Many people often confuse value creation with value addition. Adding value refers to refining something that already exists by improving its functions, features and services. This is similar to upgrading an existing cell phone with an improved camera or other feature.

Value creation, on the other hand, is synonymous with creating a beautiful carbon diamond. It is about creating something new or adding a unique twist to something existing to make it better than before. Breakthrough technologies, revolutionary software applications, artistic masterpieces, and unique business models are examples of value creation.

Value creation is about pushing the boundaries, forging new paths, and entering uncharted territory. In everyday life, however, value addition and value creation are often combined, and you need a healthy combination of both to create value for others and wealth for yourself.

Myron Golden, a successful author and entrepreneur, once said, "Money is a byproduct of being a person who creates value for other people."

Suppose you want to make more money and become financially wealthy. In that case, you must focus on creating value for others, whether in the actual sense of bringing something new to the table or refining something that already exists.

Value is a subjective and multifaceted term. It means different things to different people. Its essence is that it adds some kind of importance or value to our lives. If you do something that adds some kind of convenience, comfort, or meaning to the lives of others, you create value for them.

If you do something that provides value to others, they will most likely be willing to pay for that value. Money is the usual medium of exchange in this transaction, and as a result you become financially wealthy.

The value you offer can be an idea, a service, a product, a consultation, or advice. It can be anything that makes other people's lives easier, solves their problems, and addresses their pain points or sweet spots. The more value you create, the more money you make.

According to Myron Golden, *value creation is at the heart of wealth creation*. If you want to be wealthy, your ultimate goal should not be to make more money. Instead, your primary focus should be on creating value for others, and money should be seen as a byproduct.

The universe also responds positively to this approach. By creating value for others, you are helping people and sending positivity into the universe, which the universe responds to by giving you value in the form of wealth.

Therefore, your ultimate goal should be to become a value creator by channeling your special and unique talents, skills and potential to create something helpful for those around you. Indeed, value creators are the lifeblood of our society and economy. They push boundaries and come up with problem-solving solutions for others.

Accepting money as a form of energy is closely related to the concept of value. We often have rigid views of money because we don't see it as energy.

Money as a Form of Energy

To accept money as energy, we must recognize that it adds value to our lives. It provides a medium for exchanging resources, services, and goods. Thus, money is a symbol that quantifies the energy we share with the universe and others in one way or another.

Every time you make a purchase, you share your energy, resources, skills, or time for money. Making money through our work is a material form of the energy we have brought to our business or profession. If you are a software engineer, you use your skills in that field to make money. If you run a grocery store, the effort you put into your business is energy, and you get money as a result.

In addition, everything in this universe is a form of energy. This includes animate and inanimate objects. Everything has energy and it vibrates. Similarly, money is energy in its essence. When you begin to see money as a form of energy, your view of it becomes more positive.

Instead of seeing it as a material object or possession, you see it as flowing energy. This perception empowers you to create more money and share it with the world to give value to others. Consequently, this helps you attract more money to yourself.

On the other hand, when we associate money with negativity, such as corruption, greed, or scarcity, we involuntarily repel it.

To create wealth, you must learn to see money as a form of energy and a channel for value creation. This helps you cultivate a healthy relationship with it. In addition, we must understand that money can change our lives for the better. When you become financially wealthy, you get the means to help people more.

If someone in your family gets sick, you can help that person get good treatment for the ailment. You can also invest your money in initiatives that align with your core values and beliefs. If you are an environmentalist at heart, you can support causes that help make the environment safer and greener. If you believe strongly in creating social justice for others, you can support an organization that works toward that value.

When you see money in this light, it becomes a catalyst for positive change. You become committed to creating it and mindful of how you spend it. You consciously choose where to invest your financial resources, thereby influencing the energy that flows through your life.

Value Creation Leading to Wealth

The story of Walt Disney is a powerful example of unique value creation. He was a farm boy who drew cartoons of horses for fun. As he grew older, he tried to get a job as a newspaper cartoonist, but was unsuccessful. Disney eventually found work in an art studio as a creative who made advertisements for newspapers and magazines. He began working on commercials and developed an interest in animation. Later he started his own animation company 'Walt Disney'.

He provided people, especially children, with value in the form of animated characters and entertainment. Many of us grew up with Disney cartoons and our children love them.

Disney's story is quite inspiring. It shows that if you have a relentless spirit and create value for others, you will always get more value.

Another example is Raina Grover and Richa Grover from Hyderabad, India, who created their 1 Hair Stop brand to serve women and men who need hair extensions. They found that people with baldness and hair problems struggle with self-esteem and looking attractive. So, the sisters decided to solve this problem by creating value for those who need hair extensions. They started with 2 to 3 orders a day and now receive over 150 orders a day, generating 27 million in revenue.

Now, how do you create value for others?

Identify Personal Ways to Create Value

Creating value is easier than you think. Here is how you can do it:

First, you must begin to perceive money as a form of energy so that you can have a positive attitude toward it and create and spend it wisely. To do this, I suggest that you pay attention to all the good things that happen in the world because of those who use their wealth wisely.

Think about the work that philanthropists are doing in low-income countries. Think of the time when the entire world came together to rescue and help the victims of Hurricane Katrina. Reflecting on these and similar examples helps you to accept money as a form of energy and a means to create value for others.

Second, you need to align the energy of money with your core values. To do this, write down your core values on a clean page of your journal. Your core values are the principles that you strongly believe in and that you use to live your life in a certain way. For example, one of your core values might be honesty. Another might be minimalism.

So, if you align money with these core values, you need to be honest with yourself and anyone else affected by your use of money. Second, you would have to spend money minimally and use it to create a minimalist life for yourself. That means you'd have to spend your money wisely.

Of course, you can make big purchases, but they should have some tangible value to you and not be meaningless. If you already have ten dresses, buying another one is pointless. But that purchase would make sense if you needed an expensive computer because your coding work required it. Spend some time thinking about your core values.

Once you have a better understanding of your core values, consider how you can align them with the wealth you create and use. This approach also allows you to generate ideas for creating value for others. For example, if one of your values is to eradicate poverty from the world, you can use your wealth to support organizations that work to do so. You can also use your money to help your friends, family, neighbors, or anyone else who needs money.

Your life will seem more purposeful as you align your wealth with your core values. At this point, look for times when you cannot align your money with your core values and notice your feelings and their impact on your life. Instead of beating yourself up about it, use affirmations to realign your core values with the money and energy and try to improve.

Remember the list of personal assets we created earlier? Now you can take it out and analyze your assets. You need to identify some of your talents, skills and potential that you can use to create value for others. If you are good at math, you can teach math to children and adults. You can create a YouTube channel or even an online course. As your channel grows, you can monetize it and profit from your course. In this way, you are creating value for others and using the money and energy to increase your wealth.

Also, revisit your wealth vision and see if you have the value element built into it. I mentioned earlier that our vision should be such that it adds value to the world. If your wealth vision helps create value for others, you are on the right track. If you have overlooked the "value creation" factor and are focused solely on creating wealth for yourself, you need to rethink and positively shape it.

You also need to cultivate generosity. Generosity refers to the willingness and freedom to give and share your money, time, energy, and other resources with others. It is an important virtue of an abundance mentality, because if you have a scarcity mentality, you will be reluctant to share your resources with others.

To use the power of the Law of Attraction positively, to create value for others, and to allow money and energy to flow freely into and out of your life, you must cultivate generosity. To be generous, here are some things you can try:

Volunteer with a variety of organizations, especially those that support causes that align with your values.

Be kind to those around you and speak politely to everyone. When greeting people, smile and make eye contact to show respect.

If you see people around you struggling with something, politely offer to help. For example, if you are at a park and see a child struggling to climb the monkey bars, ask if you can help. Similarly, if you see an elderly person struggling to carry groceries at the grocery store, offer to carry the bags. When volunteering to help someone, always ask if they need your help so you don't inadvertently hurt someone's self-esteem.

Although you should not be a pushover for people and should set boundaries so that no one mistreats you, sometimes it is okay to be generous with your time and energy and go the extra mile for others.

For example, if you know a good friend is in distress and talking to you will help her, go ahead and listen with a clear intention. You may even have to cancel a few plans if she starts talking to you for hours, but this act of generosity will certainly warm her up and make you feel good.

Give generously and help your loved ones financially whenever possible. If your cousin is getting married and does not have enough money to buy food for the guests, help him out.

While being generous, never do so with the expectation of receiving something in return. Remember that generosity comes from the heart and is a wonderful way to add value to the lives of others. The more selfless you are, the more the universe will reward you.

As you do all of the above, think about how you can become a true value creator and serve the world with something unique. Creating a unique problem-solving idea isn't easy and often takes time. So keep thinking about this aspect of coming up with good ideas. Some ways to think like a value creator include

Find ways to better connect with the people you are trying to serve by using your wealth vision to find their pain points. Once you know their real problems, you can work effectively to find a solution.

Take the example of the two sisters who started a business around hair extensions. They knew the problem of their target market and came up with a unique solution. They used an Instagram community to understand their audience. Similarly, you can use social media as a valuable resource to connect with the group of people you want to serve and gain deep insight into their problems.

Second, focus on the area in which you are an expert and analyze the different products and services in that area. Think about what you can do differently to address people's problems. For example, if you work in HR, analyze the different HR products and services available. Then think about the pain points of the people who use those services and products to find the gap you can fill.

You need to elevate your skill set to become a true value creator. To do this, be prepared to invest more hours in learning and working. But remember to take it easy on yourself and maintain some balance.

Once you start working on these guidelines, I assure you there will be no turning back. If you are sincere in your wealth vision and want to create value for others and increase your wealth, you will be consistent in your efforts.

You will be truly surprised at how far you will go in life while serving others and creating more wealth for yourself.

As you begin your wealth creation journey, don't forget the importance of gratitude.

"It's not how much money you make, but how much money you keep, how hard it works for you, and how many generations you keep it for."

— Robert Kiyosaki

Chapter 9:
The Wealth of Gratitude

'In ordinary life, we hardly realize that we receive a great deal more than we give and that it is only with gratitude that life becomes rich.'
— **Dietrich Bonhoeffer**

Gratitude is the light in all of our lives. It makes our hearts happier and healthier. The very thought of being blessed makes us feel content. Frankly, it is the most beautiful form of wealth there is.

The Power and Science of Gratitude

Gratitude is a truly remarkable power. Its essence lies in appreciating what you have rather than focusing on what you lack.

When you make gratitude a habit, it changes the way you think, behave, and view yourself and the world. Simply by being grateful, you begin to feel more peaceful and fulfilled.

Gratitude can also change your perspective and behavior in difficult situations. When you cultivate gratitude, you begin to see obstacles as hidden opportunities that can help you learn and grow. Dark times immediately begin to glimmer with a ray of hope. Instead of wallowing in misery, you begin to feel grateful and hopeful.

Gratitude shifts your mindset from one of scarcity to one of abundance. Recognizing what you have in life, big or small, opens you up to more fulfillment and success.

Fortunately for those who seek logic and scientific explanations for everything, gratitude is rooted in science.

Research shows that practicing gratitude significantly benefits your mental and physical health. Studies have also found that being grateful reduces your anxiety and stress. It also improves the quality of your sleep and increases your satisfaction and happiness in life.

According to neuroscience, when you have a positive experience, your brain releases the hormone 'dopamine' in your body. It is also known as the "feel good" neurotransmitter. When you practice gratitude for that particular experience, the dopamine surge in your body increases.

It ignites a cycle of positivity, and you continue to experience the 'good' and 'happy' feelings.

Findings from an article published in The Greater Good Magazine

First, let's review how gratitude affects the brain. When you practice gratitude, you increase feel-good chemicals like dopamine and serotonin. In addition, gratitude helps in several other ways. According to an article in Greater Good magazine:

"We found that, across participants, when people felt more grateful, their brain activity was different from the brain activity associated with guilt and the desire to help a cause. Specifically, we found that when people who were generally more grateful gave more money to a cause, they showed greater neural sensitivity in the medial prefrontal cortex, a brain area associated with learning and decision-making. This suggests that more grateful people are also more attentive to how they express their gratitude.

As you can see, gratitude can promote giving and increase sensitivity in the medial prefrontal cortex, which affects decision-making. Building wealth is all about making good decisions with your money, so gratitude can help.

The more gratitude you practice, the more your brain rewards you with dopamine surges and good feelings. Over time, these happy cycles tend to produce long-lasting changes in your brain chemistry, improving your overall attitude and outlook.

The bottom line is that gratitude is magic. Cultivating it does wonders for you and everyone around you.

The Connection Between Gratitude and Financial Success

The connection between gratitude and financial success is all about the Law of Attraction. If you remember reading about the LOA earlier, you know that it returns what you send. You give it love and it sends love back to you. You give it kindness and it sends you kindness. You give it gratitude and it sends back more of that.

And with that, it gives you what you want. To be grateful for your blessings is to be optimistic about everything. You may not have much materially, but your mindset is abundant.

An abundance mindset positively shapes your behavior. You don't hesitate to share your love, knowledge, information, energy, effort, time, money and other resources with others.

You are likely to help those in need, whether emotionally, physically, or financially. You are also likely to have a generous heart that believes in giving and helping others.

When you help, love and educate others, you are constantly sending out positive vibes into the universe. You send out vibes that focus on helping others with money, kindness, love, forgiveness, time, etc.

The Universe, being of a loving nature alone, is bound to reciprocate these feelings, emotions and thoughts. As a result, it will provide you with various opportunities connected to people and experiences that will help you gain various kinds of wealth, including financial wealth.

That's how cultivating gratitude helps you achieve financial success.

Practical Exercises for Cultivating Gratitude

We have discussed in detail the theory behind gratitude and wealth. Now, let's talk about how you can harness the power of gratitude to materialize wealth of all kinds.

Gratitude Countdown

The Gratitude Countdown, created by Chris Advansun and Tamara Levitt, is a helpful exercise for cultivating and strengthening your sense of gratitude.

It is a fun activity that allows you to quickly list any ten things you are thankful for. It works best with two or more people, but you can do it alone. The exercise is in the style of lightning rounds often seen on game shows. You have less than a minute to list ten things that you consider to be personal blessings.

A good tip to increase the effectiveness of this exercise is to describe the value of each blessing. So if you say you are thankful for your pet dog, describe why. If you list your house as a blessing, explain why.

Here's how you can practice this game:

Set a timer for 60 seconds. If you have friends or family around, bring them into the game for added fun.

If you have company, have everyone take turns saying their blessing. You can write them down or say them verbally. If you're alone, that's perfect, too.

When the timer starts, quickly count ten blessings. You can even start with five blessings because you also need to describe their value. So when you say you are thankful for your job, describe how it helps you pay your bills and adds value to your employer's work.

After describing your blessings, say a cumulative thank you to the universe or whatever higher power you believe in. It can be as simple as I am grateful for all my blessings and I am grateful to the universe for bestowing them upon me.

Practice this once a day or a few times a week and you'll feel more grateful than ever. A powerful time to practice is when you are stuck in a complaining cycle and feeling hopeless.

Letter of Gratitude

Think back to the good old days when you received a letter from a loved one. How it would instantly make you happy and put a smile on your face.

It is time to rekindle that happy, contented feeling. A Gratitude Letter is the perfect technique to increase your level of gratitude.

This exercise is about writing a letter of gratitude to someone, a particular experience, a blessing, or life in general, about how it has helped you and added value to your existence.

You can send it to that person if you have addressed it to a specific person. You can also keep it to yourself, especially if you are writing in general or about an important life event.

Here's how you can work on this exercise. Think about someone who has helped you or had a positive impact on your life. It could be your parent, sibling, friend, partner, child, co-worker, neighbor, etc. Describe their influence on your life and personality in a few ways. If it is your child, you can talk about how satisfied the child makes you feel.

Also, talk about the level of patience you have unlocked after the child's birth and how the child's smile lights up your entire world. When you send it to this person, keep a copy for yourself. After a few months, you can go back and read all the thank-you notes to rekindle those loving and grateful feelings and remind yourself how blessed you are.

You can also think of a particular event in your life that has brought you value, happiness, or good memories. For example, you can write a letter about your graduation day. You can address it to your college, your professors, the universe, or your life. Talk about how your graduation journey taught you important life lessons, gave you the gift of education, and gave you the knowledge to get a good-paying job.

You can also write a general letter of gratitude for your life. Summarize the important or even mundane experiences you have had and how they have shaped your life. You can even talk about the unfortunate events but remember to put a positive spin on them.

For example, if you recently had a car accident, you can talk about it. Write about how it made you more grateful for your health and life, and brought you closer to your loved ones. Or how it rekindled your hope in the universe and made you more optimistic and courageous.

When you are finished writing, go over the letter and you will probably feel a newfound contentment.

Gather all of your letters and keep them safe. You can also post one of these letters on your bedroom wall as a daily reminder of your gratitude. While I recommend writing these letters every other day, I understand that we are all racing against time. So making it a weekly ritual is fine, but do it at least once a week.

Make a Gratitude Jar

A gratitude jar is another powerful technique to foster gratitude and encourage you to be more aware of your blessings.

Here's how to make one for yourself and your loved ones.

Take any Mason jar, empty jar of jam, spices, or peanut butter. Choose a jar large enough to hold about 100 or more paper chits.

Wash the jar thoroughly and wipe it clean. You can even create a "Gratitude Jar" label and place it inside the jar.

Place it on your dining room table, bedroom table, or work desk.

Keep Post-its and a pen in almost every room of your house, including your bedroom, kitchen, living room, hallway, etc.

As you sit down to eat, acknowledge the food on your table. Write that feeling on a Post-it, fold it, and put it in the gratitude jar.

As you cook in the kitchen, enjoy the feeling, write it on a post-it, and put it in the jar.

When you get ready for work and look at yourself in the mirror, capture that good feeling. Write it down on a Post-it and put it in your gratitude jar.

Soon your gratitude jar will begin to fill up and ooze goodness.

Every time you feel down and need a nice boost, take a note from your jar and count your blessings.

Start this ritual with your family and you will spread smiles every day.

Take Gratitude Walks

As we walk, our minds often get lost in thoughts. More often than not, these thoughts pull us away from the present moment and keep us from cultivating gratitude.

Gratitude walks offer a perfect escape from such stressful walks, re-centering your focus and allowing you to acknowledge everything around you.

Here's what you need to do:

Set aside just 10 minutes each day for a gratitude walk.

Go outside for a nice walk. You can go to a park, walk in your backyard, or just walk around the block.

As you walk, notice and appreciate different things around you.

The idea is to immerse all five senses in the walk and mindfully observe and acknowledge the different sights, sounds, sensations, smells, and textures around you.

Notice the birds chirping and be grateful for hearing that sweet sound.

Focus on the skyscrapers around you and consider the interesting dimension they add to your surroundings.

Notice the breeze blowing on your face and be grateful for it.

You just have to pay attention to everything around you, take stock of things individually, and be grateful for them.

Gratitude walks are more like mindfulness-based meditation on the go. You continue to notice things around you, understand their value, and express your gratitude for them.

When you finish your walk, you feel more positive and enthusiastic than before.

Practice Gratitude Meditation

Gratitude-based meditation is a brilliant way to relax your stressed nerves, open your heart and mind to recognize and validate your blessings, and live better in the present moment.

It requires you to meditate quietly, focus your attention on something you are grateful for, and acknowledge it.

Here's how to practice:

Find a quiet, comfortable room or corner in your home in which to sit.

Sit comfortably in any way you like. You can even lie down on the couch or directly on the floor.

Close your eyes and gently bring your attention to your breath.

Take three deep breaths, inhaling through your nose and exhaling through your mouth.

Now think of something you are grateful for. You can even focus on any part of your body and cultivate gratitude. Think of your gratitude for your legs, for helping you walk, for doing your daily chores, for giving you strength. Or be grateful for your eyes as you see the world through them. Pick any part of your body, focus on its value, and you will be amazed at how many things you have to be grateful for.

Practice this meditation exercise for about 10 minutes.

When you are finished, write down your findings in your journal. It is better to write them down in your gratitude journal that I asked you to keep earlier in the book.

You can practice gratitude meditation at any time of the day. However, doing it at the beginning of the day is a great way to start your day off on a positive note. You can also practice it in the middle of the day to revive your motivation and spirit. If you choose to do it before you go to bed, that's also a wise move, as it will give you a nice recap of your blessings, calm your mind, and relax you so you can sleep well.

Start working on these practices, and soon your level of gratitude will rise to incredible heights. In addition, continue to keep your gratitude journal to keep yourself constantly filled with happy, positive vibes.

"What we really want to do is what we are really meant to do. When we do what we are meant to do, money comes to us, doors open for us, we feel useful, and the work we do feels like play to us."

— Julia Cameron

Chapter 10:
The Role of Affirmations
in Wealth Creation

*'Attitude is a choice. Happiness is a choice. Optimism is a
choice. Kindness is a choice. Giving is a choice. Respect is a
choice. Whatever choice you make makes you. Choose wisely.'*
— ***Roy T. Bennett***

Affirmations play a monumental role in manifesting your
desires, wishes and aspirations. They also effectively help you
create and accumulate wealth.

Let us discuss the science behind them, their origins, and
techniques for practicing affirmations and visualization.

The science behind affirmations and visualization is very
similar. The two are closely related practices, so if you
understand the mechanics of one, you'll easily understand the
other.

Let's begin by discussing affirmations in this chapter and
visualization in the next.

Affirmations and Their Origin

Affirmations are statements that you believe to be true. It can be anything you accept as truth and believe in. An affirmation can be positive, negative, or neutral. We refer to positive affirmations when we discuss using affirmations to create wealth or achieve your goals.

To affirm something in your mind, you must focus on it. We often repeat the things or statements we want to focus on, which is an effective and common approach to practicing affirmations. This is why practicing affirmations is also known as chanting mantras.

The Science Behind Affirmations

The science behind affirmations is fascinating and multifaceted. First, both visualization and affirmations, also known as positive affirmations, operate on the premise of the Law of Attraction, which states that you attract to yourself whatever you focus on most, be it positive or negative.

So when you focus on positive images, thoughts and statements, you attract positive experiences, opportunities and results, including abundance and wealth. Conversely, if you focus on negative beliefs and thoughts, your chances of attracting negative experiences increase.

Another important aspect of this equation is the RAS, which stands for reticular activating system. This is a system in your brain that prevents information overload by eliminating unnecessary information. This keeps your brain from holding on to unnecessary and meaningless information so that it doesn't exhaust you.

Your criterion for filtering out extraneous information from important information is based on emotional involvement and repetition. If you are emotionally involved in an experience or hold a belief very dear to you, it will stick in your mind. Your RAS perceives it as important.

The same thing happens when you say something repeatedly. Affirmations are most often practiced by chanting the statement you want to embed in your mind. So when you chant a suggestion over and over again, your RAS accepts it as something important and doesn't filter it out of your system.

A good example of this is when you start thinking about losing weight, you come across different workout plans, fitness regimens and diets. Similarly, if you keep drilling wealth-based affirmations into your mind, eventually your subconscious will accept them as your beliefs and then rewire you to think about them more.

That's when LOA kicks in and manifests your desire by sending more of what you send out into the universe.

Studies show that repeating affirmations helps your brain create new neural pathways. These pathways form physical connections to the thoughts you repeat. As these pathways strengthen, your mind finds it easier to return to the positive statements and thought patterns instead of falling prey to negative thinking. This leads to fruitful physical and mental results associated with positive thoughts, including prosperity-based affirmations.

To harness the power of affirmations to create wealth, you must create wealth-based affirmations and rewire your mind to think positively about wealth. The affirmations take some time to have their full effect, but the results begin to pour in. Belief is an integral part of this process, so you must fully believe what you are affirming.

Affirmations have worked wonders for many people before you and in your time. Let's discuss some examples to give you more confidence in the power of affirmations.

Success stories that demonstrate the power of affirmations

From celebrities to show hosts to self-help gurus to actors to athletes to business people, everyone loves affirmations and uses them to unleash their full power to achieve their goals.

Here are some success stories of people who attribute a large part of their triumphs to affirmations.

Oprah Winfrey

One of the most successful women in the world, Oprah Winfrey is an activist, host, philanthropist, actress and celebrity. She is a firm believer in affirmations and strongly attributes much of her success to her affirmation practice.

Winfrey began practicing affirmations when she was very young. She would create positive affirmations and say them to herself every day. By embedding these affirmations in her mind, she was able to successfully handle and overcome many of life's adversities and slowly climb the ladder of success.

Tony Robbins

Tony Robbins has made a name for himself in the world of coaching, motivational speaking and personal development.

He has empowered millions of people with the ability to believe in themselves, and he knows for a fact that affirmations have been instrumental in his success and that of those he has helped.

Robbins practices affirmations religiously every day of his life and continues to use their power to shape his life the way he wants it.

Arnold Schwarzenegger

Arnold Schwarzenegger is an incredibly successful actor and businessman. The former governor of California has achieved remarkable success, and he attributes much of it to affirmations.

Schwarzenegger says he used to regularly tell himself, "I am the best" and "I will be successful. The more he practiced these affirmations, the more confident he became. His self-belief helped him make informed decisions and fruitful choices that led to his victories.

These stories clearly demonstrate the tremendous potential of positive affirmations. Many other stories prove the same, but the book limits me to sharing just a few.

My point is simple: if affirmations have helped many people, they can do the same for you. The ball has been and always will be in your court: it is time to pick it up and throw it hard.

Now let's discuss how you can create effective wealth-focused affirmations and harness their full power.

Creating Effective Wealth-Focused Affirmations
Barbara Hannes Howett once said, "Just when the caterpillar thought its life was over, it became a butterfly.

Your life may have seemed to be in shambles at one point, and it may have seemed like there was nothing left to do or to improve. But if you believe in the power of the universe and in yourself, you can emerge victorious at the end of every turmoil. You too are a beautiful butterfly. You just need to recognize and accept your power to fully unleash it.

Creating powerful affirmations is easy. You just need to take care of a few details and factors and you will successfully create transformative affirmations for yourself.

The process below highlights each step you should take to make this happen. We are talking specifically about wealth-based affirmations, and you can use the exact same process to create all kinds of affirmations designed to achieve different goals, such as being healthy, following your passions, achieving professional success, building happy relationships, finding your soul mate, gaining confidence, and the like.

Let's begin the journey.

Start by getting clarity about the kind of abundance you want. You can create affirmations to achieve any type of wealth. However, to get the results you want, it is best to focus on one type of wealth at a time, create an affirmation based on it, and practice it. You can practice several wealth-based affirmations daily, but try not to mix them up to avoid confusion.

You can also create columns for different types of wealth and a few affirmations for each.

Before you create your affirmations, you need to know your exact goal for each type of wealth. To be truly wealthy and abundant means that you are trying to attract and manifest all kinds of wealth: financial, physical, social, emotional, psychological and intellectual. So you must have a goal for each of these.

Think about what kind of social wealth you want and why. What amount of annual or monthly income would make you happy? Why do you want to be intellectually wealthy? As you ponder these questions, you will begin to have clarity about the kind of wealth you want in each area. For example, your financial wealth goal might be to earn $20,000 every month. Your goal for social wealth might be to have a loving relationship with your nuclear family.

Now you need to create a positive (P), present (P), and concise (C) affirmation for it. I call this the "PPC" formula. A positive affirmation should be free of words with a negative connotation, such as no, not, won't, couldn't, and the like.

Avoid making suggestions such as "I won't spend time alone and will socialize more" or "I don't want less money" or the like. The human mind has a design flaw that omits negative words, rephrases the suggestion, and focuses on that. So if you say, 'I won't be sad,' your mind will probably change it to 'I will be sad. Your suggestion must be purely positive, so you are feeding your mind positive mental food.

Second, your suggestion should be concise so that it is easy to repeat and mentally consume. Keep it between five and ten words at most. There's no harm in having longer suggestions, but it's hard to remember and repeat them often. If a longer one works for you, go for it.

Third, it should be present-oriented. Your suggestion should state your goal as if you have already achieved it. Instead of saying, "I want to be happy," say, "I am happy. I want to be happy' is an example of a future-oriented suggestion, suggesting that you want to be happy in the next few days.

The problem with future-oriented suggestions is that they confuse your mind. It is trying to bring you happiness in the future while you remain deprived of it in the present moment. A present-oriented suggestion, on the other hand, focuses on helping you achieve your goal in the present. I am happy' suggests that you are happy here and now.

Your mind then shifts your attention to things that can bring you happiness and encourages you to manifest your present goal. So if you want to earn $20,000 a month, your affirmation should be, "I am earning $20,000 a month.

Once you have created your affirmation, you must practice it. You can say it out loud, write it, or do both at the same time. Write each word slowly, focusing on it as you absorb it emotionally and mentally. Write it at least five times-more is better.

You can write as many times as you want, but you must practice consistently to make it a habit. So start by writing it five to ten times a day. When you get the hang of it after a few weeks, you can write it 15, 20, 25 times or more. Again, it's not necessary to write it even five times on every occasion, especially when you're first working on building the habit.

When you say the affirmation, you must do so slowly, loudly, and confidently. Say each word slowly so that it rings in your ear and you focus on it. Your voice should be loud enough so that you can hear the affirmation and pay full attention to it.

Finally, say your affirmations with complete conviction. Yes, say it like you mean it. The stronger your belief in the affirmation, the easier and better your mind will accept it. Once your mind accepts it, it shapes your belief system accordingly, influencing your behavior and actions. And that's how you begin to create and accumulate the kind of wealth you want.

Go ahead and follow the above outline to create wealth-based affirmations. You can also use some of the following powerful affirmations to attract, create and accumulate wealth in your life.

I attract prosperity, wealth, and abundance towards me.

I always have sufficient money.

I am worthy of social, emotional, financial, and intellectual wealth.

Money flows towards me easily. (You can replace money with friends, wisdom, talent, etc.)

My life is full of wealth.

I easily save money.

I easily create wealth.

I am excellent at managing my money.

I am excellent at increasing my wealth.

Abundance surrounds me.

I easily make money.

I attract good fortune.

Work on these affirmations or use them as a foundation to create your own: the choice is yours. Just remember the PPC formula and make sure you practice your affirmations twice a day. You will get better results if you do it once in the morning and once before you go to bed.

The affirmations shared above are generally about the healthy concept of wealth. You can and should create specific affirmations that focus on your goals for the different types of wealth discussed above.

Integrating Affirmations into Daily Life

Your next task is to integrate your affirmations into your daily routine. This isn't a very difficult task. You just need to take care of a few things and work on a few practices, and soon your affirmations will have a permanent place in your daily life.

Here's what you need to do:

Set a reminder to practice affirmations when you wake up. You will probably be groggy when you wake up, so you only need to say the affirmation once or twice. Please don't force yourself to write it down at this time, as this may annoy you enough to make you want to stop the practice before it becomes a habit.

After you eat your breakfast, write your affirmation five times. If possible, chant it at the same time.

Set another reminder to practice your affirmation around noon and then one before you go to bed. You need to practice it for a few minutes about three to four times a day.

It is better to do it alongside an existing habit so that the existing habit serves as a reminder for your new habit. For example, if you write affirmations after eating breakfast, your breakfast will serve as a reminder to write your affirmations. If you practice deep breathing before going to bed or getting under the covers, tie your affirmations to that practice so that the first habit reminds you to say your affirmations each time you take a deep breath before going to bed.

To fully integrate your affirmations into your routine, you must let go of your skepticism and put every ounce of your faith into the practice. To do this, you must always speak positively to yourself. When you speak positively to yourself, you build positive self-talk, which encourages you to think optimistically. Soon you are rewiring your brain to think about hope and abundance. When this happens, you automatically begin to let go of any skepticism and fully believe your affirmations.

Second, surround yourself with positive people. When you are surrounded by positivity, you block out negative vibes that might interfere with your belief in your affirmations.

Third, pay attention to the small improvements and blessings in your life that you might otherwise ignore. For example, if a friend gives you a gift, that is a blessing and an abundance. Appreciate it and be grateful. If you meet someone who seems like a good professional contact, be grateful for that connection. Observing and acknowledging such small but meaningful blessings helps you to believe that you can attract abundance and prosperity. As a result, your belief in your affirmations is strengthened.

In addition, visualizing what you are saying or writing down is a brilliant way to strengthen your belief in your affirmations.

"I love money. I love everything about it. I bought some pretty good stuff. Got me a $300 pair of socks. Got a fur sink. An electric dog polisher. A gasoline powered turtleneck sweater. And, of course, I bought some dumb stuff, too."

— Steve Martin

Chapter 11:
Visualization:
Picturing Abundance

'Visualization is daydreaming with a purpose.
— Bo Bennett

Visualization is an immensely powerful tool that can help you attract and manifest wealth and abundance. Much like affirmations, visualization empowers you to think positively.

In this chapter, we'll take a deeper look at what it is, how it works, and how to practice visualization.

What is visualization?

The Power of Visualization
Visualization is the use of imagery to create mental images that rewire your mind to think a certain way. Also known as creative visualization, it is a cognitive process of creating clear and detailed mental images.

Have you ever had someone tell you to visualize a scenario and immerse yourself in it? Say you were to imagine that you were in a meadow with a beautiful stream bubbling on one side and birds chirping in the sky. If you close your eyes and imagine this scenario, this is visualization in practice.

Visualization gives you the power to think and imagine anything you want. You can consciously add and change the images you want and do anything and everything with your mind's eye.

When you visualize your desired results or goals, you can transform yourself and your life.

How does visualization work?

The science behind visualization is pretty much the same as the science behind affirmations. Like affirmations, visualization uses your cognitive ability to visualize what you want. When you repeatedly visualize a scenario with certain actions and elements, you encourage your mind to think in that direction.

Your RAS is also activated and you consider this visualization important. This particular imagery becomes part of your belief system and reframes your thoughts and behavior in that direction. You project positive thoughts into the universe and use the power of the Law of Attraction to send desired opportunities and experiences your way.

As you visualize the future as you want it, you gradually create it. An important point to remember is that our minds cannot distinguish between imagination and reality. If you tell yourself something over and over again, you will eventually believe it, even if it is not reality.

Think of a time in high school when you heard a rumor several times. Chances are that you eventually believed it without digging into the truth and discovering the reality. Perhaps years later you discovered that the story you believed in high school had no basis in fact. Even though it was fictional, you believed it. You heard it many times, so your mind confirmed the story.

Second, when we hear a story, we often visualize it by creating mental images. By repeatedly thinking about an incident or story, the images become embedded in our subconscious memory bank. Once it's embedded in our mind, we believe it, and so it becomes part of our belief system.

Similarly, you can use visualization to your advantage. Instead of believing superficial stories and fabricated rumors, you can use your mind's obliviousness to reality to make it believe the good things you feed it. When you feed your mind positive mental food in the form of creative imagery, you use its ability to believe to help you achieve your goals.

You can visualize yourself becoming wealthy, achieving all your financial goals, being surrounded by love and happiness, having beautiful relationships, being skilled and talented, having the wisdom and intellect to ace life and handle adversity, and fulfilling your ultimate purpose in life.

Repeatedly feeding your mind such visualizations focuses your attention on your goals. You activate your RAS, send positive thoughts into the universe, and use the LOA to send great opportunities. That's how you use visualization to attract wealth and abundance.

Now, let's discuss some successful examples of people who practice visualization and attribute their success to it, so you can better understand its power.

Case Studies on the Power of Visualization

Visualization is a constant in the lives of many people, including the successful people we admire and seek inspiration from. Here are some success stories of those who attribute their triumphs, success, and wealth to visualization.

Jim Carrey

Jim Carrey's journey as an actor hasn't been a smooth one. In the 1990s, he struggled to get work and good roles.

He began using visualization to help him get through the tough times. A popular story is that he once wrote himself a check for $10 million for acting services, dated 1994. He carried this check in his wallet every day and used it for inspiration.

Finally, in 1994, he got a role in Dumb and Dumber for which he earned $10 million. It was his daily visualization practice that helped him achieve his goal.

Kerri Walsh and Misty May-Treanor

Historically, Kerri Walsh and Misty May-Treanor have been a successful and renowned women's beach volleyball duo.

With three glorious Olympic gold medals to their name, the duo believe that visualization, yoga, and meditation have played a large role in their success. In a recent interview with USA Today, Walsh mentioned that they both practice visualization a lot. In her words, "A lot of what we do is visualization. Being able to take in the sights, sounds, stress, and excitement will help us move forward.

Her inspiring story is further proof that visualization works like a charm.

Lindsey Vonn

Vonn is one of the most successful and famous female skiers of all time. According to the incredible gold medalist, her mental practice helps her stay ahead of the game.

In an interview, she said, "I always visualize the run before I do it. By the time I get to the starting gate, I've already run the race 100 times in my head, and I'm imagining how I'm going to make the turns. I love that exercise. Once I visualize a course, I never forget it.

The interesting thing is that she not only creates mental images known to physically simulate the course. She constantly shifts her weight as if she were skiing and practices breathing patterns as she visualizes.

Visualization is indeed immensely powerful and helpful. It has been an effective tool in empowering many people and can do the same for you. Let us focus on how to practice visualization and how to incorporate it into your daily routine.

Basic Visualization Exercise

The basic visualization exercise is very simple. All other visualization techniques and exercises flow from it.

Here's what you need to do to perform it.

Sit comfortably in a quiet room or place. You can even lie down if you wish.

Take a few deep breaths to clear your mind of unnecessary thoughts.

When you feel calmer, take another deep breath and center yourself.

Now think about the wealth-centered goal you want to achieve. For example, if you want to become a millionaire by running your own interior design company, and you want to have several branches, you can achieve that goal.

Now imagine that your design business is doing very well. Name it to encourage the universe to help you manifest this dream.

Create a mental image of your store with customers pouring in. Imagine your sales going through the roof and you making millions. Imagine yourself planning to open another store in another city.

Enliven your imagination by adding sights, sounds, colors, and expressions. The more details you include, the more you immerse yourself in the visualization.

Think about this scenario with your eyes closed for about 10 minutes. You can even set an alarm to start.

After ten or more minutes, gently move toward ending the exercise. Imagine that everyone is applauding your efforts and you are getting the recognition you have always wanted. You return to your beautiful home and have a wonderful time with your family.

Now gently open your eyes and enjoy this incredible fantasy. Enjoy it for a few moments.

If you wish, write down how this exercise made you feel.

Say a nice thank you to the universe or whatever higher power you believe in for giving you this experience. In this way, you combine visualization with gratitude and send even more positive vibes into the Universe, which the Universe will return in abundance.

Make this a daily practice. Do it at least once a day. Stack it on top of your affirmation practice or an existing habit that you never break, such as taking a shower or drinking coffee in the morning.

This strategy helps you easily incorporate visualization practice into your routine and make it a lifelong habit.

How to Create Your Vision Board

A vision board is a helpful way to lay out your vision and map out your goals. It is a visual representation of your hopes, dreams, and aspirations.

You post pictures, clippings, and images relevant to your dream on a board and reflect on them daily. It is a creative visualization practice that helps you immerse yourself in the experience and focus fully on the wealth and abundance you wish to manifest.

Here's how to build it: Take a whiteboard, canvas, or even a large piece of chart paper in any color you can easily find.

You can also create a vision board on the back of your bedroom door.

Now think about the goal you want to achieve. For example, if you want to be the CEO of your company, find pictures of yourself after a promotion or of successful people in magazines. You can even take a picture of your current CEO and put it up with a picture of you. If you want to be a famous author, draw a picture of a book and add your name as the author. Or add pictures of published and successful writers.

You can add as many pictures as you like. You can also get prints of motivational quotes that inspire you and place them on the board.

Write your goal at the top of the vision board. Print it out and add the clipping to your vision board when you have time.

You can add more pictures, quotes, and goals every day.

It is best to have a vision board dedicated to one or more big goals with smaller goals.

Spend 5 to 10 minutes each day looking at the board and visualizing yourself achieving all of your dreams.

Soon you will be thinking more about your goal and slowly moving closer to achieving it.

Immerse all 5 senses in your visualization

Our senses are one of our greatest assets. Unfortunately, not many of us realize this. Visualization becomes even more powerful when you bring it to life. An incredibly effective way to do this is to immerse all five of your senses in the experience.

Think of a time when your sense of sight, touch, hearing, taste, and smell were fully involved in an experience. Perhaps it was the first time you ate spaghetti and meatballs and enjoyed it so much that you ate it with your hands. Or the time you graduated from college and could feel and smell the victory you basked in.

When you engage your five senses in any experience, you can experience it fully. You become fully involved in the experience and successfully embed it in your subconscious mind. Once your subconscious accepts the experience, your conscious mind becomes more focused. You begin to actively work on the goal and soon achieve it.

Here's how to use your five senses in visualization:

As you visualize your goal, gradually include your five senses in the visualization.

Think about how the people in the experience look. Think about your dressing habits: the clothes you are wearing, your appearance, the smile on your face. Are you standing in your brand new office? Are you opening a new branch of your business? Add as many colors and textures to your imagination as you can.

Next, think about what your success smells and tastes like. What would it be like to associate a taste and smell with success? Will it taste sweet or a mixture of salty and sweet? As for the smell, perhaps you have smelled the scent of a successful person you once met and can associate it with your success.

Similarly, focus on the sounds you hear. Perhaps people are cheering or applauding you. What are the sounds like? What cheers do you hear for yourself? Are they calling your name?

Next, think about the things you can feel. Maybe you are shaking your sponsor's hand. What does it feel like? Imagine touching your new office, table, chair, and other things in your imagination, and focus on how the textures feel on your hand.

The more sensory details you add to your imagination, the more your goal will feel real and attainable.

Continue this practice for 10 to 15 minutes.

When you open your eyes, you will feel accomplished and happy. Cherish this good, satisfying feeling and hold on to it. Use it to stay inspired and actively work toward your goal. You will begin to make the necessary efforts to bring your vision to life.

Sketch Your Aspirations and Goals

If you have a knack for creativity, you can turn your goals and ideas into meaningful art. That creative visualization technique immerses you in the experience, energizes your mood, and makes the practice fun.

You can simply make pencil sketches of your goals. Draw yourself, the surroundings you are in, and the goal you have achieved.

You can use visual tools such as <u>Clickup Whiteboards</u>[1] to create digital drawings of your goals and roadmap.

Build on the drawings daily and color them to make them more believable.

You can practice this exercise even if you aren't artistic at heart and are terrible at drawing. Who cares if your doodles aren't pretty? The idea is to engross yourself in the visualization and make it a part of your routine.

Whenever you sit at work, you can draw a little 'success' doodle, focus on it for a few minutes, and then start your work after chanting your affirmation. You'll be amazed at how productive you become after this quick practice.

Carry Out Mental Rehearsal

Mental rehearsal is a very popular and commonly used visualization technique, especially among Olympic athletes.

If you have seen any videos of famous skier Mikaela Shiffrin, you would have noticed how she practices mental rehearsal

---

[1] <u>https://clickup.com/features/whiteboards</u>

before every race. Her eyes are closed, and she moves her body while simulating skiing up and down a slope.

It helps if you adopt the habit of doing the same. Initially, it can feel funny, so you consider doing it alone. Soon, you'll get the hang of it and find it rather enjoyable than silly.

Here's what you need to do:

When you visualize achieving a goal, also think of the steps you must take and write them down or make mental notes.

Then imagine yourself doing all those things. For instance, if you are visualizing opening your cafe, think of how you are buying different supplies and equipment for it. Imagine getting up from your chair and visiting stores to buy stuff for your bakery.

Next, get up and start enacting that entire experience.

In your daily routine, whenever you are about to work on a task, think about it first and visualize yourself doing it. If you are writing a report, imagine opening your laptop and then drafting your report. Now, think of how you are typing away every word and finalizing your report. This technique also incorporates visualization into your daily routine and helps you stick to it.

You now have lots of practice to work on. Pick anyone that feels the easiest and start exercising right away. Take it one technique, one day at a time, instead of rushing through the practice and trying to do everything simultaneously.

"Wealth consists not in having great possessions, but in having few wants."

— Epictetus, Greek philosopher

Chapter 12:
Adopting the Wealthy Habits of Rich People

'Ninety-nine percent of the failures come from people who have the habit
of making excuses.'
— **George Washington Carver**

Like any other goal, wealth and abundance will not be handed to you on a silver platter, accompanied by a magical spoon that feeds you. Like most things, you have to work for it.

Yes, having a vision, a strategy, and an action plan is great, and it works. But you need something more. You need to adopt positive habits that are conducive to creating wealth and abundance.

Humans are creatures of habit. Our daily routines and lives are full of good, bad and neutral habits. The goals we achieve, the results we get, the experiences we have, and the setbacks we often encounter are also the result of various habits.

To become financially wealthy, you must cultivate the habits of financially successful and wealthy people.

Let's discuss these habits, along with strategies for incorporating them into your daily life.

The Wealthy Habits of Rich People

Focus on Continuous Learning

Successful people understand the importance of continuous learning. They know that it is their most valuable asset. To use that asset effectively, they are constantly learning and growing.

Financially successful people have a learning mindset. You will find them constantly studying and learning. They know that their skills and abilities affect their earning potential. Therefore, they are constantly acquiring new skills to expand their skill set. Not only that, but they also believe in increasing their awareness of everything in the world, because you never know when a particular piece of information or knowledge might come in handy.

Case studies that demonstrate the transformative power of this habit

Many people have used this habit to transform themselves and their lives. Examples of wealthy and famous people who have done this include Warren Buffet and Bill Gates. Bill Gates used to spend an hour every night reading. Buffet, on the other hand, spends about six hours a day reading.

Both believe that their commitment to continuous learning has been a key factor in their success.

So how can you build this habit and integrate it into your daily life?

Strategies for integrating this habit into your daily life

Here are some powerful strategies that can help you develop the habit of continuous learning and growth:

Start by reading books that are relevant to your field, your goals, and your vision for wealth. A quick online search can provide you with many resources on any topic. Find those books, pick 3 to 5 top ones or ones you feel connected to, and start reading them. If you can, get hard copies of the books. Otherwise, PDFs or e-books can work just fine.

Start by reading 3 to 5 pages of a book each day. Stack this practice on top of an existing habit so it fits easily into your routine.

Reflect on what you read and think of ways you can apply what you learn each day. For example, if a book asks you to be curious about the world, explore things deeply.

Make a list of the influential or wealthy people you admire or consider your idols and start following them on social media. You will learn a lot from their personal experiences and stories.

Stay up to date on policies and regulations relevant to your field so that you are compliant.

Find and use the various technological tools and software that can help you advance in your work. Try to automate as many processes as possible, rather than always relying on yourself or active manpower. Use human resources for research and development and for inventing innovative solutions.

Join various study and mastermind groups of influential people, both online and offline. Such groups help you learn from the experiences of others and develop beneficial collaborations.

Begin this practice and you'll be amazed at how much you grow mentally and emotionally in a matter of weeks.

They Live Within Their Means

Successful people don't become financially wealthy overnight. They invest a lot of time, effort and energy. One of their habits is to plan ahead for their financial needs and follow a budget. This habit comes from their principle of living within their means.

They analyze their basic needs, monthly expenses, and income. They then create a budget that they follow throughout the month and stick to it with discipline.

This strategy helps them avoid unnecessary spending, so they save a good chunk of money and use it to invest in themselves, their passion projects, and their industry.

Financially successful people know that if you make a dollar every day, you cannot spend two dollars every day. They understand that if they make twenty-five thousand dollars, they have to live on twenty-two or twenty-three thousand dollars. If you make forty-five thousand, you have to limit yourself to forty thousand.

For many people, this may seem difficult. I have known people who had huge incomes, but were broke because they used to spend way beyond their means. And I personally know very rich people who spend very wisely. Even when they can afford extravagance, they stay away from it.

Case studies that show the transformative power of this habit

Elon Musk's life is one of the most remarkable examples of this habit. With a staggering net worth of $195.1 billion, Musk is known for his intense work ethic. He does not believe in having a lavish lifestyle, living in a two-bedroom apartment and working long hours. He has a fixed budget that he religiously follows and invests all of his earnings in his projects SpaceX, Tesla, X, Neuralink, Open AI, and the like.

Moreover, if you read Rich Dad, Poor Dad by Robert Kiyosaki, you'll notice how he talks about some significant habits of rich and poor people. In the book, Kiyosaki talks about two different mindsets: the mindset of the rich and the mindset of the poor.

Now, those he calls poor in the book are people who make a lot of money and those who have a great social reputation. However, their focus is more on portraying themselves as rich and conforming to the superficial social norms of being more, having more, and doing more.

On the other hand, those who are truly rich shun these values, pay more attention to growing their wisdom and finances, and live lives of purpose. They often earn more than the poor in the short term, but become more financially stable in the long term.

Strategies for integrating this habit into your daily life

To be financially wealthy, you must also teach this practice. Here's how to get there:

Analyze your monthly income and expenses.

Make a list of all your income streams, if you have more than one. Subtract taxes from these to determine your net income.

Now calculate all your expenses, including essential and unnecessary ones.

Look at your basic expenses and your monthly income and create a monthly budget. If your basic expenses exceed your income, you need to reduce them or increase your income.

Set a weekly and daily spending limit according to your budget.

For about six months, try to live as simply as possible. Cook your meals at home, don't eat more than you need, don't buy extra clothes or things, and cut back on trips and events. It will take a few months, but eventually you will start to follow your budget and limit your spending.

Also, analyze and write down your daily expenses. Look at your daily and weekly budget every day to remind yourself to stick to it. If you go over it, figure out what expense broke your budget. Also, challenge yourself to make amends the next day. For example, if your daily budget is $100 and you spend $150 on Tuesday, you will have a budget of $50 for Wednesday.

While you are doing all of this, set aside a certain amount of money for your savings. You can either have a monthly savings goal or put $5 to $20 or even more into a savings jar every day. You can even have weekly savings milestones where you try to save $50 (less or more is fine, depending on your unique situation) each week.

As your savings grow, think of ways to invest them. A common practice among successful people is to use their savings for goals and projects tied to their vision, as Musk does. You can do that, and you can also find some investment streams to grow your funds.

Following a strict budget can be challenging and sometimes make you feel limited. To fulfill your vision, you have to do that. The first three to four months will seem difficult, and then you will get the hang of it. Also, once you see the positive results of this habit, you will be more interested in saving as much as possible and sticking to your budget.

They Practice Good Time Management Skills

Time is a limited resource. Many of us often run out of it. If only we had more than 24 hours, we could get so much more done" is a thought that resonates with many of us. When there is a lot to do, we often find it easy to run around in circles, not accomplishing anything substantial.

Well, this is another thing that separates us from financially successful people. They are more organized and make excellent use of their time. They believe that time is money and one of their most valuable resources. As a result, they use it effectively and efficiently without wasting it.

Using a variety of practices, they analyze their important tasks, assign them to specific times of the day, and actively work to accomplish them. To be financially successful, you must develop good time management skills.

For this particular habit, I'll share the various time management practices you can use to manage your time well, along with examples of successful people who have practiced these exercises and transformed their lives as a result.

Strategies for Incorporating This Habit into Everyday Life (with Case Studies)

Some of the best time management exercises that can help you make the most of your time are

Set a consistent bedtime and wake-up time, and start your day as early as possible. You have more time if you wake up around

5 or 6 in the morning. You have enough time to focus on yourself and work on important tasks. Richard Branson, one of the richest men in the world, has a strict habit of waking up at 5:00 a.m. every day to work out.

He believes that working out early in the morning increases his productivity, keeps him fit, and allows him to make the most of his time. So set a bedtime and wake-up time that allows you to get 6 to 8 hours of sleep each night. Wake up early, dedicate some time to your well-being, and then get started on your important tasks.

Make your daily to-do lists, identify the important tasks from the crowd, and get to them first. Always prioritize your important tasks first, especially those that will dramatically increase your productivity. American author and entrepreneur Tracy Anderson is a true practitioner of this rule.

She always takes notes, distinguishes the important tasks from the unimportant ones, and discards the latter. She then visualizes herself doing those tasks and gets right to work.

Eating an ugly frog first thing in the morning is an analogy that Brian Tracy uses to encourage people to tackle their most difficult and annoying tasks. Eating an ugly frog refers to doing the most difficult task first thing when you get up. There's nothing more disgusting than eating an ugly frog. But once you imagine doing it, you can do anything else.

Similarly, once you do a deadly task, you know you have the strength to do anything and everything else. As a result, both your motivation and your productivity increase. The night before the next day, identify your most difficult task and tackle it the next morning. You'll be amazed at how relieved you feel when you get it done, and how much your productivity improves just by taking care of that one task.

It can be difficult to tackle a big task right away. That's why you need to break it down into smaller, more manageable pieces so you can tackle it seamlessly without overwhelming yourself.

Break your big task into small steps and spend 20 to 30 minutes on each step or mini-task. Take short 5-minute breaks between each work segment. Also known as the "Pomodoro Technique," this is a good time management hack that can help you finish difficult and annoying tasks without dragging them throughout the day. It was created by Italian chef Francesco Cirillo, who used a tomato-shaped timer to complete his tasks on time. A timer to practice this technique is a good idea, but you can practice it without one.

Start by delegating tasks to others that you're not an expert at or that don't require your first-hand attention. The truth is that we cannot do everything ourselves. The sooner we **accept** that, the easier it will be to manage our time well.

Bill Smith, founder and CEO of Shipt, is a firm believer in the power of delegation. He knows the importance of delegating certain areas of his work life so that he can focus on those that require his most attention. When you create your work calendar, identify the tasks you can outsource and delegate to someone else or your team members.

For example, hire a laundry service instead of doing your own laundry. Instead of checking your email and responding to clients and vendors, hire a virtual or physical assistant to handle those tasks.

Start with at least one of these practices and gradually add the rest to your routine. Set reminders on your phone to follow these practices, and you'll build the habit in a few weeks.

Seek Passive Income Options

Passive income refers to the money you get from income streams that you do not actively invest time and effort in. You're not actively working in that stream to produce results.

Wealthy people know that they cannot put 100% of their time, effort and energy into everything and grow their income. They also know that they need more than one income stream to grow their finances. With this in mind, they maintain one or two active income streams and several passive income options.

Typically, they use their savings to invest in passive income streams.

Case studies that demonstrate the transformative power of this habit

Jasmine McCall is a 32-year-old mom and the founder of Paybump. She quit her recruiting job at Amazon, which paid her a six-figure salary, to launch PayBump and grow her YouTube channel.

McCall creates videos about unique income streams and remote work. She also makes kits to help people improve their cover letters and resumes. She sells her digital products through her blog. She currently earns $143,000 a month between her YouTube ad revenue and digital product sales. The icing on the cake is that McCall only works two hours a day.

Strategies for incorporating this habit into your daily life

If you want to be financially wealthy like Jasmine McCall, you need to work on creating some profitable passive income opportunities for yourself. Here are some steps to help you do that:

Research different passive income streams you can try. Some good ones include creating digital products, blogging, affiliate marketing, investing in stocks, and buying real estate that you can later rent out.

Start by investing some of your savings in the passive income options you like best. Do your research so you know how long it will take you to break even and how much you will need to invest.

A smart approach is to contact someone who has successfully built a business using the income stream you are considering. You can find these people on Reddit, Facebook groups, Instagram communities, and Quora.

Another approach to starting a passive income stream is to partner with a friend, relative, coworker, or social acquaintance who is already earning from a lucrative passion income option. For example, if a friend runs a successful blog that generates over $5,000 per month, you could invest in her business.

Be patient with whatever passive income stream you choose, because nothing becomes successful in two weeks.

Once your current passive income business becomes stable and generates a decent income, create another passive income stream. Use your wealth vision and goal to create 4 to 5 passive income streams that generate approximately $20,000 to $50,000 per month.

When you find someone to partner with, look for a passive income opportunity that plays to one of your skills and expertise and produces income with little to no input from your end.

Have a healthy wealth and life balance

It may sound strange to you, but the wealthiest people in the world have a sense of wealth/work/life balance. While many of them are workaholics, that doesn't mean they ignore their personal lives and don't engage in activities that bring them peace, joy and comfort.

Devoting yourself to your work only interferes with your health and well-being. If you push yourself to work long hours, don't rest, or don't take time for yourself, you're heading for burnout. Countless people have experienced severe burnout that has even landed them in a hospital bed.

You don't want to go through that ordeal, do you? In that case, you need to develop the habit of maintaining a healthy work-life balance. It is a habit because you have to train yourself to work and not worry about anything but your well-being for a while.

Case Studies Showcasing the Transformative Power of This Habit

Ev Williams, co-founder of Twitter, is a firm believer in a healthy work-life balance. He advises everyone to take care of themselves, because if we don't sleep well, don't exercise, eat unhealthy foods, and run on adrenaline for too long, our performance will suffer. Our performance, in turn, affects our decisions and our business. So it is important to have a balanced life and to love those close to us.

Facebook's COO, Sheryl Sandberg, leaves the office at 5:30 every day so she can be home for dinner with her kids, and she has done this regularly since she became a mother.

Strategies for integrating this habit into your daily life

Creating wealth and life balance can be a little tricky, but with the following guidelines, you can achieve this goal:

There are different ways to balance work and wealth, and different things work for different people. One approach is to work some days with time for sleep, eating, and some routine activities, and then not work some days.

This strategy works well for many people who find it difficult to work, rest, and have fun in the same day. Another approach is to schedule a few hours of work each day and two to three hours of relaxation and leisure. The third approach is to work at your usual pace and take the weekends off completely. You can also dedicate one month a year to a solid vacation, with weekend getaways in between.

So, the first step is to figure out which approach seems most beneficial and feasible to you. Analyze your personality, lifestyle, work ethic, wealth vision and goals to determine the strategy that works best for you.

Next, you must motivate yourself to create a wealth-life balance. First, create an intention to do so. Your intention can be something like: I have and will maintain a healthy wealth-life balance,' or 'I will work hard and also create enough time to relax. Read and chant this intention (a positive affirmation) daily to drill it into your mind and activate your RAS to take it seriously.

Second, look for the signs in your health and life that indicate the need for work-life balance. Some of these signs include:

- Getting sick too often
- Not getting enough sleep each day
- Severe headaches
- Family and loved ones complaining that you never have time for them
- Feeling extremely anxious, depressed, or chronically stressed
- Feeling despondent
- Feeling that your life is about work and not about you
- Feeling lost and chaotic in the midst of work
- Struggling with nausea, indigestion, or other health problems
- Taking too many medications

If you have two of these signs and symptoms, you don't have work-life balance. Think about how these problems will only get worse over time and make you feel even crazier. Think about the many beautiful and simple moments of joy that you are letting go of and how you are missing out on so much that life has to offer.

Use these signs as a source of motivation to think about and work for your well-being. Chant your intention once more and then move on to the next step.

Now figure out how to balance work/wealth and life. Once you have decided, create a plan to achieve it.

Your schedule should be such that you get 6 to 8 hours of work each day with some time to rest. If you want to have a daily rest period, find a window of time that will allow you to do so. You need to do things that bring you joy, satisfaction, and peace during this time. You could paint, listen to your favorite music, work on a new hobby like baking or dancing, watch a movie, or do anything else that makes you happy.

If you decide to set aside certain days/months for work and certain days/months for leisure, figure that out and put it on your calendar. These vacation months or weekend getaways would motivate you to work hard during your work weeks/months to have your reward in the form of relaxation and vacations.

If you have a family, you can even plan these things with them because it is important to consider their wishes.

I understand that creating a work-life balance can take some time, but if you are fully committed to it, you will achieve this goal as well. Remember that being ambitious is fantastic. You should have ambitions and pursue them. But don't do it at the expense of your well-being.

The Role of Discipline and Consistency in Developing New Habits

Building any new habit requires discipline and consistency. You cannot get away with not working on either if you want to develop and maintain the many positive habits discussed above and throughout this guide.

Discipline refers to sticking to what's right and required of you and behaving according to the guidelines or standards of a particular task or goal you're trying to achieve. In terms of the habits you are trying to build, discipline is not giving in to your temptations, but working on the habits every day.

Consistency refers to the quality of doing things or behaving in a certain way. It means that if you want to create a daily budget and stick to it, you have to do it every day of the week. If you are going to journal your thoughts daily, you must do it every day.

If you do not have self-discipline, you will find it difficult to be consistent in developing certain habits. And the more consistent you are, the stronger your discipline will be. When you do a certain daily practice, you build a routine. This routine encourages you to stay true to the practice while fighting your temptations.

Here are some ways to strengthen your discipline and become consistent in developing the necessary habits:

Create an environment that supports the development of your habits. Remove things and elements from your space that can lure you to your temptations.

Continue to affirm these habits throughout the day. For example, if you are trying to save money, you might say, "I find it easy to save money" or "I sleep on time.

Now, Identify your triggers and work to manage them.

In addition, if you work on the practices I shared earlier in the book, such as setting goals, stacking new practices on top of existing habits, and setting reminders, your ability to stay disciplined and consistent will only improve.

"There is no monopoly on becoming a millionaire. If you're jealous of those with more money, don't just sit there and complain—do something to make more money yourself."

– Gina Rinehart

Chapter 13:
Conclusion–Your Wealth Journey

'Every great story happened when someone decided not to give up.'
— Spryte Loriano

You have finally reached the end of the book. Let's recap what you've learned and give you some tips on how to apply what you've learned in this book to your everyday life.

Summary of Key Lessons
Wealth is more than just money. It has social, emotional, intellectual, psychological, physical, and spiritual dimensions. To become truly wealthy and abundant, you must focus on becoming wealthy in all of these areas.

Cultivating an abundance mindset is critical to creating wealth. An abundance mindset focuses more on sharing your resources with others, while a scarcity or limitation mindset focuses on lack and hoarding.

You need to reflect on yourself to determine if you have a scarcity mindset and then work to change it to an abundance mindset.

Identify your strengths, virtues and talents to determine your assets. You can then use them wisely to create wealth, fulfill your vision, and create value for others.

Create a wealth vision to know exactly what you want and to give more meaning to your life.

Cultivating gratitude is critical to creating wealth. When you are grateful, you use the Law of Attraction to send more good things and opportunities your way.

It is important to identify the limiting beliefs that keep you from creating wealth and replace them with growth-oriented beliefs.

Affirmations and visualization are powerful tools to help you manifest your desires. Use their power every day to move closer to your wealth-related goals.

Just as important as working and achieving your wealth vision is taking care of your health and personal life. Maintaining a wealth-life balance is essential to staying healthy and happy.

Focus on creating value for others and being generous with your knowledge, time, energy and money.

Money is a form of energy. When we recognize it as such, it begins to flow better into our lives.

Be sure to align your values with your vision of wealth and the money to achieve your vision, and use your money wisely.

Tips to Implement This Book's Key Lessons in Your Life

When you come across a tip or strategy, think about how you can practically add it to your life. For example, if you read about social wealth, think about what's missing in your relationships and work on that area.

Go slow to stay steady. Don't rush through any step or practice. It is best to focus on the biggest pain point in your life and improve that first, and then once that area is in a healthy place, you can turn to improving the other areas. For example, if you are struggling to maintain good health, read the sections on creating good physical health and work on those strategies first.

Be sure to record what you do to track your progress.

Reflect on your journey every day, or if that's not possible, at least twice a week.

Approach life and your journey and read this book with an open mind. There may be things in this book that conflict with your views and beliefs. Analyze them respectfully and objectively and see if they make sense. Similarly, on days when you are too hard on yourself, keep an open mind and treat yourself with kindness and respect. Doing so will make it easier for you to move forward and improve.

This book isn't just words to me. It is me pouring out every lesson I have learned in my life to empower you. You are full of potential and power, and you may not realize your power right now, but as you work to unleash your full potential, you'll be amazed at how awesome you are.

I always want you to remember that you can do anything you put your heart and mind to. So if you commit to creating wealth the right way and truly empowering it, you will surely succeed in that goal.

I also want to sincerely thank you for taking the time to read this book. You have played a pivotal role in helping me achieve my vision: to help people empower their wealth. For that, I am extremely grateful.

I hope this book proves to be a beacon in your life and continues to guide you towards a life of abundance, wealth and prosperity.

All the best to you and your financial abundance,

Scott Allan

"At least eighty percent of millionaires are self-made. That is, they started with nothing but ambition and energy, the same way most of us start."

– Brian Tracy

References

1. Choosing Therapy. Scarcity Mindset. Retrieved from https://www.choosingtherapy.com/scarcity-mindset/

2. Grabianowski, E. . How Fear Works. HowStuffWorks. Retrieved from https://science.howstuffworks.com/life/inside-the-mind/emotions/fear3.htm

3. Matz, S. C., Gladstone, J. J., & Stillwell, D. (2016). Money Buys Happiness When Spending Fits Our Personality. *Psychological Science*, 27(5), 715–725. https://doi.org/10.1177/0956797616635200

4. Headspace. There Will Always Be More: Overcoming Scarcity Mindset. Retrieved from https://www.headspace.com/mindfulness/there-will-always-be-more-overcoming-scarcity-mindset

5. Ogola, E. Understanding the Impact of Scarcity Mentality on Personal Growth. LinkedIn. Retrieved from https://www.linkedin.com/pulse/understanding-impact-scarcity-mentality-personal-growth-ogola-1qaaf/

6. Jude, M. How Great Leaders Communicate Big Vision So That Others Want To Join In. Medium. Retrieved from https://medium.com/@Jude.M/how-great-leaders-communicate-big-vision-so-that-others-want-to-join-in-d3296e7ca37e

7. Daltrey, S. What Is Wealth Psychology? LinkedIn. Retrieved from https://www.linkedin.com/pulse/what-wealth-psychology-stephen-daltrey/

8. Kothari, P. Wealth Chapter 2: Types Part 1 - Intellectual. LinkedIn. Retrieved from https://www.linkedin.com/pulse/wealth-chapter-2-types-part-intellectual-priyank-kothari/

9. Kothari, P. Wealth Chapter 2: Types Part 4 - Emotional. LinkedIn. Retrieved from https://www.linkedin.com/pulse/wealth-chapter-2-types-part-4-emotional-priyank-kothari/

10. Mark. Gratitude: Your Path to Success and Wealth. LinkedIn. Retrieved from https://www.linkedin.com/pulse/gratitude-your-path-success-wealth-mark/

11. Vocal Media. The Power of Visualization and Affirmations in Manifesting Wealth. Retrieved from https://vocal.media/lifehack/the-power-of-visualization-and-affirmations-in-manifesting-wealth

12. Lawrence, K. The Power of Visualization: Invoking Wealth, Health, and Happiness. LinkedIn. Retrieved from https://www.linkedin.com/pulse/power-visualization-invoking-wealth-health-happiness-keith-lawrence/

13. Mindbodygreen. Successful People Who Use the Power of Visualization. Retrieved from https://www.mindbodygreen.com/articles/successful-people-who-use-the-power-of-visualization

14. Benchmark Wealth Management. 4 Ways to Align Your Money With Your Values. Retrieved from https://benchmarkwealthmgmt.com/4-ways-to-align-your-money-with-your-values/

15. Griffiths, D. Money is Energy: Understanding the Energetic Aspect of Wealth. LinkedIn. Retrieved from

https://www.linkedin.com/pulse/money-energy-understanding-energetic-aspect-wealth-dean-griffiths-q1k6e/

16. CNBC TV18. How these two sisters from Hyderabad are earning Rs 27 crore a year by selling hair extensions – 1 Hair Stop. Retrieved from https://www.cnbctv18.com/startup/how-these-two-sisters-from-hyderabad-are-earning-rs-27-crore-a-year-by-selling-hair-extensions-1-hair-stop-17860051.htm

17. Kim, L. 11 Most Famous Entrepreneurs of All Time and What Made Them Wildly Rich. Inc. Retrieved from https://www.inc.com/larry-kim/11-most-famous-entrepreneurs-of-all-time-and-what-made-them-wildly-rich.html

18. Alimi, T. Adding Value Vs Creating It: Unlocking Doors To Wealth. LinkedIn. Retrieved from https://www.linkedin.com/pulse/adding-value-vs-creating-unlocking-doors-wealth-tale-alimi-jjv5f/

19. Ferework. Beyond Money: The Art of Creating Value and Wealth Generation. LinkedIn. Retrieved from https://www.linkedin.com/pulse/beyond-money-art-creating-value-wealth-generation-ferework/

About Scott Allan

Scott Allan is an international bestselling author of over 30 books published in 16 languages in the area of personal growth and self-development. He is the author of **Fail Big**, **Undefeated,** and **Do the Hard Things First**.

As a former corporate business trainer in Japan, and **Transformational Mindset Strategist**, Scott has invested over 10,000 hours of research and instructional coaching into the areas of self-mastery and leadership training.

With an unrelenting passion for teaching, building critical life skills, and inspiring people around the world to take charge of their lives, Scott Allan is committed to a path of **constant and never-ending self-improvement**.

Many of the success strategies and self-empowerment material that is reinventing lives around the world evolves from Scott Allan's 20 years of practice and teaching critical skills to corporate executives, individuals, and business owners.

You can connect with Scott at:

scottallan@scottallanpublishing.com

https://www.scottallanpublishing.com/

www.scottallanbooks.com

Also Available by Scott Allan

PATHWAYS TO MASTERY SERIES

Visit www.scottallanbooks.com for more deals on book bundles and merchandise to build your great life.

PATHWAYS

TO

BY SCOTT ALLAN

MASTERY

THE SERIES

www.ingramcontent.com/pod-product-compliance
Lightning Source LLC
Chambersburg PA
CBHW021425180326
41458CB00001B/139